Baseball's back in town

CMC

A Controlled Media Corporation Publication

12 Bedford Road, Toronto, Ontario, Canada M5R 2J8

Baseball's back in town

By Louis Cauz
Design Ralph Tibbles

Dedicated to Alberta Mae Eldridge
and Luciano Cauz, my parents.

Acknowledgments

Let me offer my grateful thanks to a great
number of people who assisted me in record-
ing the facts and supplying the photographs
on which this book is based. They include:
Robert L. Hunter, Mary Pollock and family,
William L. Bell, T. B. Lawson, Bill Houston,
Gordon Kirke, Peter Carnegie, Bill McMurray,
Harold Roberts, Ernie Miller, Marty Green-
berg, Mike Filey, John Moore, George Wil-
liams, Joe Wright, Michael Burns, Dave
Crichton, Joe Crysdale, Henry Roxborough,
Jean Sterling, R. Falconbridge Cassels, Jack
Muir, Scott Young and Smitty – Bill Smith.

Above all, however, I wish to express my
deepest gratitude to Clifford Kachline, historian at the National Baseball Hall of Fame and
Museum, Gordon Walker, Bobby Hunter Jr.,
David Rhydwen and his Globe and Mail
library staff, and my former editor, James
Vipond.

Prologue: Why Toronto's history?

Why a book on the history of organized baseball in Toronto?

It had been only a minor league town. The old Leafs had gone bankrupt. The stadium had been torn down. All true. But the fans were still here.

They read the box scores and probable pitchers, watched the Game Of The Week with Garagiola and Kubek, or took weekend trips to Montreal for Expos' doubleheaders.

The city did have a great baseball tradition. The fact that so many people cared showed in the intense excitement on the day it appeared the San Francisco Giants were headed for Toronto. The Giants didn't reach Toronto but the American League and the Blue Jays did a few months later – and all over southern Ontario baseball fans rejoiced.

Baseball was back in town. Suddenly our baseball past was important.

Hubbell, Grimes, Gehringer, Kiner, Keeler, Brouthers, Lajoie, Duffy and Barrow had worn Toronto uniforms.

Two men analyzed the situation perfectly.

Donald McDougall, president of Labatt Breweries of Canada and the man who played the major role in bringing the big leagues to Toronto, spoke to the Board of Trade.

"Baseball in Toronto has a storied past that we should resurrect because a generation of Torontonians do not fully appreciate it," he said. "Toronto can and should be proud of its baseball tradition."

Gordon Walker's statement some time earlier was equally significant. Walker, who worked for the ball club in the 1940s and spent many years with The Globe and Mail before joining the Canadian Football League as its director of information, said, "I hope that when major league baseball arrives – I mean when they're right here on the field – that the people who bring it won't think they need diagrams to explain the game to Torontonians.

"What Toronto has in quantity is baseball tradition. Memories are made of this."

Tradition, a colorful past, and memories. Okay. But it was fragmentary. Some of it was myth. Research had to go beyond newspaper files to baseball history locked away in attics, basements and drawers of old cabinets. Hours of reading microfilm exposed errors which had been magnified and compounded from one era to another.

Numerous trips were made to the National Baseball Library in Cooperstown, N.Y., home of the Hall of Fame. The Central, Municipal Reference and The Globe and Mail libraries were invaluable for checking the spelling of players' names and obscure statistics – neither of which were considered vital at the minor league level in the pre-1900s.

Records of runs batted in and earned run averages were not kept for a number of years.

A letter from a relative solved the spelling of club president James Johnstone McCaffery's often mis-spelled last name.

All of this research has produced a book that may at times wander and does not pretend to cover everything.

You won't read about Mickey Sinks, a discontented Toronto pitcher, letting the air out of the tires of league president Tommy Richardson's car by mistake. He thought it was the plate umpire's car. Or other unforgettable characters.

It does not purport to be the definitive history of baseball in Toronto. This task would involve several volumes. But this is the most complete account of the subject yet assembled.

We hope that this book, in pictures and text, will settle a few arguments, put a myth or two to rest and give Toronto's newest generation of baseball fans a hint of what Toronto's baseball past was all about. Then we can all watch what lies in the future, with a new crowd of players and characters.

Louis Cauz

– Louis Cauz

Origin: Sorry Abner, the English beat you to it

Ask a baseball historian how many games Moonlight Graham played for the New York Giants in 1905 and you will get the answer in a second.

"One; and he never went to bat."

Simple!

Everybody remembers Ol' Moonlight, the outfielder from down Fayetteville way.

But ask the same authority and nine others about the origin of baseball and you will get ten different replies.

You will hear about archaeologists discovering on the walls of Egyptian temples drawings which depicted human figures playing ball more than 40 centuries ago.

There is a ball in the British museum, a leather sphere without A. G. Spalding's autograph, which was knocked into the Nile about 2,000 B.C. You will be told of legends that the Chinese, Hindus and early North American tribes indulged in the sport. And that the French played a game in the 12th century with four milking stools as bases.

The most popular theory is that the game was invented by the English and was called "rounders," a children's game.

The game was brought to America by early settlers who called it various names, including Town Ball.

About the only point historians agree upon is that Abner Doubleday DID NOT invent the game one afternoon in 1839 by explaining the rules and laying out a perfectly geometric playing field for fellow West Point cadets in Cooperstown, N.Y.

It is a fact that the game of baseball (or "base ball") appeared in print as early as 1700 and was played in America before and during the Revolutionary War. Also, the rules of baseball attributed to Doubleday in 1839 were identical to those in a rule book for the English game of "rounders" published in London in 1827.

Wells Twombly, in his book "200 Years of Sport in America," says that the greatest American baseball myth, starring Doubleday, never occurred.

"There is absolutely no evidence that Doubleday invented the game. On the contrary, an enormous amount of literature shows, rather clearly, that the General (he was a noted Civil War general) had nothing to do with

baseball. Surely a man who kept as careful an account of life as Doubleday did would have recorded his love of baseball, yet of the 67 diaries in the possession of Doubleday's heirs not one volume mentioned the sport.

"In the post-Civil War era, when baseball was presented to the nation as professional entertainment, the General did not even acknowledge its existence, odd behavior for the man credited with inventing the game."

He died in 1893, long after baseball had become popular. It certainly was something worth boasting about, but Honest Abner went to his grave without saying a word.

Still, baseball's establishment, especially Spalding, the U.S. sports equipment man who made millions putting his name on baseballs, needed an originator, preferably a red-blooded American – not an Englishman.

Spalding formed a distinguished committee to fight the suggestion that baseball was a foreign import and in 1908 Doubleday was posthumously anointed as father of baseball.

Spalding's insistence that the game was contrived in the United States alienated his close friend Henry Chadwick, an Englishman who lived most of his life in Brooklyn and was baseball's pre-eminent pioneer writer. As chairman of the rules committee he introduced changes which shaped the present game.

Chadwick, baseball's first statistician, invented the box score and wrote the first rule book.

Nevertheless, Albert Goodwill Spalding, one of the game's great pitchers and later a manager and owner, had the last word on baseball's origin for many years until better evidence refuted the claims of the 1905-1908 commission.

What about the game's origin in Toronto? This seems to have occurred in the late 1850s. Baseball had been played in cities and towns close to the U.S. border and by that time was gradually gaining acceptance in southwestern Ontario centres.

In 1859 the Toronto Globe reported: "A number of young men in this city have organized themselves into a baseball club called the 'Canadian Pioneers'. They practice every Monday afternoon at 4 p.m. on the University Grounds."

General Abner Doubleday did not invent baseball...but he never claimed he did. Hall of Fame is located in Doubleday's home town, Cooperstown, N.Y.

9

However, for many years the game was not highly regarded by the better class of Toronto citizens. Lacrosse was at its height of popularity. Players, strict amateurs, were from leading families and anxious to establish lacrosse as the national game of Canada.

Baseball was an importation from the United States, a fact sufficient in the eyes of some to make it a questionable game. One writer of the period said, "Cricket is for elders; lacrosse is for younger socialites; but baseball is just a sandlot sport, usually played by undesirables."

The Dauntless and Clippers were early Toronto teams and in 1874 the Dauntless team (formerly the Pioneers) was privileged to play one of its games on the "sacred" precincts of the Toronto Cricket Club. They beat the Aetnas 55-22.

The Clippers, however, were the stronger team. They practised, by permission of City Council, in Queen's Park, northeast of the Parliament Buildings.

Skilled and popular with the public, the Clippers in 1876 joined a group known as the Canadian Professional Baseball League, which included teams from London, Guelph, Markham, Port Hope and Kingston.

Professional in that era often meant competing for $10 stakes rather than being dependent upon gate receipts for income.

Canada's first "professional" league folded after one season but London Tecumsehs and Guelph Maple Leafs survived to join the International Association, which historians claim was baseball's first minor league. It didn't claim to be a major league like the National Association, which folded in 1875.

In joining baseball's first minor league, London and Guelph played against teams from Pittsburgh, Columbus, Lynn, Mass., Rochester and Manchester, N.H. The Tecumsehs surprised by winning the title in 1877. But both London and Guelph were out of the first minor league within two years.

In 1876, a year after the death of the National Association, the National League, the first truly professional baseball league was founded. It still exists today.

As baseball continued to grope for acceptance in Ontario the game was also spreading in the 1870's from the United States into Quebec and the Maritimes and out to Winnipeg and the prairies. The New York Knickerbockers toured Montreal and Toronto, playing both lacrosse and baseball against local teams.

In the 1880s cricket was beginning to wane in popularity. Fans discovered that baseball was an excellent game to wager on, and the betting added an extra dimension of excitement.

An Englishman, visiting Montreal in the 1880s, wasn't overly impressed with the game. In a letter to friends in England he wrote: "Baseball is difficult to understand. The fielding is infamous. Catches, my dear, which a village team would have secured were missed over and over again by these champions and no one seemed surprised.

"Almost all the players are professional and there is a very serious competition for the services of any exceptionally good man, while betting on the various teams runs very high. Amateurs are rare in the extreme – at least, so we are informed by a Canadian gentleman with whom we travelled."

Baseball was then in its transitional era. Prior to 1881 the ball was pitched underhand, batters were allowed one base on a hit and were out if the ball was caught on one bounce. Players were bare-handed.

There were no strikes or balls until 1858 and a soft bouncy ball made of India rubber was used. In 1880 a batter got four strikes and a walk was given after eight balls. In 1881 the pitcher's box was moved back five feet to 50 feet (it's 60 feet, 6 inches now) and pitchers could throw overhand, taking only one step before delivery.

By 1883 it was apparent that the businessmen of Toronto were anxious to get the city back into organized baseball. The impetus was surprisingly supplied by James McKinley, who at the time had never pitched a full game in practice or in a match, but was a natural athlete.

Pitching for the Clippers, by then better known as the "Torontos," McKinley and the touring team went to Guelph and upset the champion Maple Leafs, 1-0.

Toronto was ready for organized baseball.

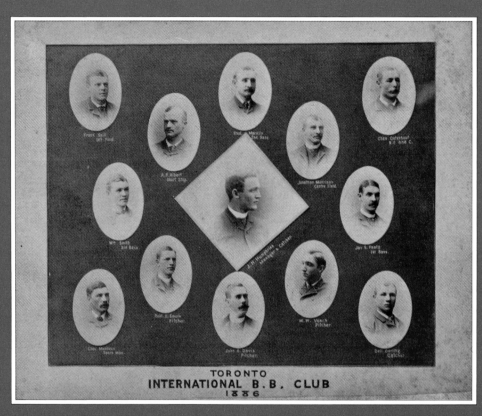

Frank Spill   Fred Macklin   Charles Osterhout
August Alberts   Jon Morrison
William Smith   John Humphries   Jay Faatz
Robert Emslie   W. W. Veach
Charles Maddock   John Davis   Del Darling

1885–1889

Organized baseball arrives and so does Cannonball

The year was 1885 and Toronto newspapers published casualty reports of the battles raging at Duck Lake and Batoche's Ferry in the North West Territories.

Khartoum was under siege and a feature in The Globe described the city of Cincinnati as the "Paris of America" where the people "gave themselves up to pleasure seeking."

Louis Riel, the young radical who led the Red River Rebellion, was in jail in Regina. The jury recommended mercy and the government of Sir John A. Macdonald was accused of an act of inhumanity when Riel was hanged.

The newspapers also carried reports of a meeting of Toronto businessmen at the Rossin House (later the Prince George) to discuss the formation of a baseball club.

It was proposed that a joint stock company be formed to operate a team in the Canadian League, which had teams from London, Guelph and two from Hamilton. Strongly supporting the idea were ex-Alderman Thomas Hunter, later elected president, Peter Ryan, E. Strachan Cox, Deputy Police Chief Stark, William Macpherson, Lem Felcher and E. T. Malone.

If a good club can be put together here large numbers of people will attend the games, they said.

"Last year's experience proves this; but last year was the first time that any interest of any account was taken by the public in the game, and if a club which can hold its own against any in Canada can be formed, and the general public begin to understand the points in baseball (which comparatively few in the city do as yet) then the attendance at the games will equal that of first class lacrosse matches."

Deputy Stark thought the enterprise should be viewed in a commercial light, and for this reason the players should be paid and subject to strict discipline.

He said it would cost about $2,500 to operate the club for a year and thought the plan most advisable would be incorporation of a joint stock company having 500 shares at $10 apiece.

A motion was passed to this effect with shareholders putting down 20 percent and the remainder upon call. It was felt that 20 home games, including six on Saturdays, would produce enough revenue to operate the club successfully.

The team organizers decided to play their games at the Jarvis Street Lacrosse Grounds, which could be "secured" for $100 per month with the privilege of using it three days a week for practice or match purposes.

The club declared it would import a playing manager from the United States and no more than four players from Toronto would be invited to play.

The manager was Harrison L. Spence, 29, of New York, who later managed Indianapolis of the National League. Spence, a second baseman, had Sandy Reid, a London, Ont., boy who had played in the majors, at short, Fred Macklin at first, F. L. Smith in right and McKinley, the local boy, pitching and at third.

The Torontos of 1886, the city's first International League team. The man in the diamond is manager-catcher John Humphries. The two fellows to his right are batting champion Jon Morrison and Jay Faatz, the "elongated first baseman who could take them out of the clouds." Directly below is the pitching staff—Bob (The Wig) Emslie of Guelph, later a great National League umpire, John (Daisy) Davis and W. W. (Peekaboo) Veach.

His main performers, however, were to be Theo Scheffler, Tom O'Rourke and Bill Stemmeyer, imports.

All later played in the National League.

The Torontos, with Scheffler pitching and O'Rourke catching, lost their first game in organized ball, 3-2 to the Guelph Maple Leafs in 12 innings. But McKinley gave Toronto its first league win, 12-9 against Hamilton Primroses at Dundurn Park.

On June 5 manager Spence had his "ball tossers" out for a practice for the club's home opener, June 15.

The largest crowd ever to witness a baseball match in Toronto (if not the largest ever assembled at the Jarvis and Wellesley Street grounds) turned out to see the Torontos take revenge on the Maple Leafs, winning 8-5.

Reporting in those days was flowery and descriptive. One story went: "The Torontos were confident of winning from the start, and although the Leafs took the lead in the first inning, and kept it until the sixth, they never evinced any disposition to show the white feather, but stuck to their work and at the end of the seventh inning had the game well in hand.

"The Guelph boys played a very plucky game, and took their defeat like men, without any kicking or wrangling with the umpire, thus setting a good example to several other Canadian clubs."

It was remarked that "the ladies did not turn out as well as was to be expected, but they will soon learn to appreciate a good game of baseball."

Substitutes were not then permitted in this period unless the opposition agreed. Twice Guelph requested a sub, once for Purvis when he injured his finger and again when Ross had his thumb knocked out of joint.

Spence objected, and after a doctor put the "afflicted member in its natural position" Ross went to rightfield.

Scheffler, winning pitcher, received solid support as his team made "only" 12 errors. The Guelph team made 23, including 11 by Purvis.

Stemmeyer, a big fellow from Toledo who mystified batters with a pitch called the curve ball, made his debut a couple of games later and pitched a no-hitter in a contest in which there were 22 errors. He beat Hamilton Clippers 6-4.

That first season Toronto finished a commendable third, winning 24 of its 44 games, and the club awarded diamond pins to Scheffler, O'Rourke and Spence. Stemmeyer and McKinley, who each won 10 games, were ignored. In Toronto the team's third place finish was considered a disgrace. The city wasn't accustomed "to this sort of thing" said one writer. (See accompanying article.)

The season, however, was a success financially. Players' salaries were $4,231, gate receipts $8,500.

The Canadian League, which had paid $50 to gain recognition as a member of organized baseball, had its entry fee returned when the American Association refused to adhere to some of the bylaws of the National Agreement governing the major and minor leagues.

Toronto, it soon became apparent, would not be satisfied playing against smaller nearby cities. It wanted to expand into the United States for competition.

A. G. Spalding, the baseball equipment magnate from the United States, was seeking to expand his company's business horizons when he paid a visit to Toronto in February of 1886.

Spalding suggested that Toronto apply for a franchise in the National League and immediately set visions of grandeur in motion. Toronto didn't make it to the National League, but less than three weeks later it was announced that Toronto and Hamilton would forsake the Canadian League and join Syracuse, Rochester, Binghamton, Buffalo, Utica and Oswego, members of the New York State League, to form the International League.

The league changed its name on several occasions during the next 34 years but the merger of the two groups was the founding of the minor league of which Toronto would be a member (except from 1891 to 1895) until its last club went bankrupt in 1967.

There was criticism of Toronto's move but the Hamilton Spectator in an article, February 24, 1886, defended the shift, saying "professional baseball is a pure matter of business. Large salaries are paid to the players and heavy expenses are incurred in the management of the teams."

Copyright 1888.
Goodwin & Co. N.Y.

Ned (Cannonball) Crane did everything but take tickets at the gate in 1887. He hit .428, won 33 games (including two on the final day of the season) and played in the outfield.

Copyright 1888.
Goodwin & Co. N.Y.

SLATTERY, L.F. NEW YORK'S

Note the shoes on Mike Slattery, the base stealing champion of 1887. His 112 thefts for Toronto is still an International League record.

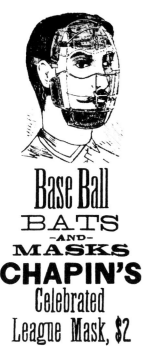

Base Ball
BATS
-AND-
MASKS
CHAPIN'S
Celebrated
League Mask, $2

"Money must be forthcoming or the thing cannot go on. The ball team cannot live on sentiment. It cannot exist on the friendship of Guelph with a deficit in the gate receipts. Business is business and in baseball, as in everything else, owners are as much entitled to look out for number one as any other class of businessman."

A U.S. magazine also noted Toronto's success following the 1885 season, stating: "The American national game greatly prospered in Canada, at least in the province of Ontario, where the British element of the population of the Dominion largely prevails.

"In the French Canadian district manly sports of the field, like baseball and cricket, do not flourish as they do in Upper Canada. As for Canada, baseball is rapidly obtaining a foothold with both cricket and lacrosse."

Early in 1886 construction on the first park built specifically for baseball in Toronto was underway on eight acres of land south of Queen Street and adjacent to the east bank of the Don River. Cost of the buildings and ground work was $7,000.

The main entrance was on Queen Street with exits for visitors in carriages on Eastern Avenue, Kingston Road and Scadding St. The covered grandstand, which was in the shape of a half octagon, had a seating capacity of over 2,000 with a 550-seat reserved section in the middle.

The seats had arms, cushions and comfortable backs. A wire netting protected fans from stray balls. A spectator was charged 10¢ above the 25¢ admission for entrance to the grandstand and an extra 10¢ to sit in the reserved section.

Directors decided to charge these prices to "ladies as well as gentlemen and to have no 'ladies days' as was the custom the year before."

The grounds were bounded by a "close smooth-board matched fence, which will tax the acrobatic talent of the smartest youth to surmount," and had sliding doors on the south, east and west sides which "would be used by the players to recover the ball when it is hit over the fence, which is not likely to happen very often."

In its early years the park was known as the Toronto Baseball Grounds. Later writers re-

ferred to it as "Big Wood Smith's place over the Don," and "the beautiful park over the classic Don."

The enclosure, however, was best known as Sunlight Park, because of its proximity to Sunlight Soap Works (Lever Bros. Ltd.).

A small dead-end street west of Broadview Avenue now commemorates the park with a marker high on a lamp post announcing that this is Baseball Place. There is also a very small bit of parkland at the Eastern Avenue turn-off to the Don Valley Parkway marked Sunlight Park.

John H. Humphries, a catcher, was the Torontos' new playing-manager for its initial season in the newly formed International League. A large contingent of local fans took the train to Rochester for the league opener, May 10, 1886.

Arriving in the early hours of the morning they "began skirmishing about town in quest of speculators desirous of backing the Rochester nine."

The Torontos appeared in maroon caps, shirts and breeches with gold belts and stockings. John (Daisy) Davis pitched a four-hitter and the Torontos won 6-4.

It was noted that the Torontos had acquired a "very small and very fat colored boy" in Syracuse who traveled with them as their "mascotte."

The presence of this boy, Willie Hume, on the Toronto bench was protested in Buffalo after the Torontos had won a pair of games. Buffalo, however, went out and secured a "young colored boy to sit on its bench to offset the good influence of Willie Hume," who the night before had received four ovations for his mouth organ playing at the Adelphi Theatre.

The Torontos' first home games in 1886 were played at the Rosedale Athletic Grounds because the new field wasn't quite ready. But on May 22 the Torontos were host to the Rochester Hop Bitters at their new park.

The game, played before more than 3,000, was described, "as fine a game of ball as the most critical of baseball enthusiasts could wish to see. All classes of society, from the Lieutenant-Governor to the omnipresent newsboy, were represented. A more impartial gathering never beheld an athletic contest of any kind."

It was pointed out that the game was watched and appreciated "with an understanding that was surprising considering the short time that has elapsed since baseball first became a popular sport in Toronto."

W. W. (Peekaboo) Veach allowed three hits in a 10-3 win and everybody was happy, "from the fat mascot in his gaudy suit to the president (E. Strachan Cox) of the association. A fine silk hat belonging to one of the Governor's party was roughly treated by a foul ball."

That year Peekaboo Veach and Daisy Davis were the team's top pitchers along with Guelph's Bob (The Wig) Emslie, who later gained fame as a big league umpire and pitcher.

Jon Morrison in centrefield was the league's leading hitter, batting .353 and scoring 107 runs, also tops, for the Torontos. Other able men included Jay Faatz, the "elongated first baseman who could take them out of the clouds," and William Smith.

Toronto finished third behind Utica and Rochester but in 1887 won its first league championship with a powerful club which included the multi-talented Ned (Cannonball) Crane, who won 33 games and led the league in hitting with a remarkable .428 average.

When Cannonball wasn't pitching he was used in the outfield or at second to utilize his hitting ability. Considered the fastest pitcher in baseball at the time, he won 16 in a row and gave Torontos the pennant by winning both ends of a doubleheader on the final day of the season.

Crane also had a "deceptive drop ball which was a puzzler" and at one time held the world record for long distance throwing. He went up with New York and Cincinnati teams and won 76 games before returning to Toronto in 1895.

Catching Crane and the club's other top pitcher, "Doc" Sheppard, were Harry Decker, later credited as inventing the catcher's "Decker" glove, and George Stallings, who gained fame in 1914 as manager of Boston's "Miracle Braves."

August Alberts and Mike Slattery also batted over .350 and Slattery set two records, one of which still exists, as he stole 112 bases and scored 134 runs. His stolen base mark has never been equalled in the International League.

A 12-team league, before Utica and Oswego dropped out part way through the 1887 season, the group changed its name to the International Association in 1888 and Toronto finished second to Syracuse.

Charlie Cushman, who had taken over the team in 1887, lost most of his top players the following season. But he came up with a talented replacement for Crane in Albert Atkisson, who had been a 25-game winner and twice pitched no-hitters for Philadelphia.

Atkisson, like Crane, won 33 games for Toronto and led the league in strikeouts with 307.

Stolen bases had been in the box score for three years and the Torontos had another leader in Eddie Burke, an outfielder who stole 107 in 1888 and another 97 in 1889. Burke went on to an outstanding National League career.

Though the Torontos finished out of the first division in 1889 they had an interesting team. Catcher Deacon Jim McGuire, who went on to manage Washington, Boston and Cleveland, became the first Toronto player to clout three homers in a game.

The team's first home run champion was Bill Hoover, who hit 10 (a considerable total in the "dead ball" era), and also scored 114 runs while hitting .333. Toronto that year ran up one 36-5 score in beating Toledo as Tom McLaughlin scored six runs.

The pitching staff consisted of three men – Tom Vickery (20-22) who led the league in strikeouts and walks; Bill Serad (19-16), whose wildness prompted legislators to introduce the hit batsmen rule because he hit so many hitters; and Ledell (Cannonball) Titcomb (14-13), who went up to the majors the following year and pitched a no-hitter.

It was an ever changing era. Umpires were allowed to seek advice from players and even spectators. Occasionally a manager or player acted as umpire. Umps also gave players five minutes to recover a lost ball. The supply was short.

WILLIAM SMITH

3rd Baseman of the Toronto Base Ball Club. Fatally Injured while bathing on Hanlan's Island, Toronto, August 8th, 1886. Died Monday, August 9th, at 3.30 A.M.

"God rest his soul in peace."

The death in 1886 of third baseman Smith prompted officials to hold a benefit game. Fans were urged to retain the $1 souvenir ticket. "Don't give up this ticket at the gate. Keep it in memory of the honest player, for the benefit of whose Mother it is issued" was the message on the back of the ticket.

George Stallings, former medical student and Toronto catcher in 1887, gained fame as the hot-tempered genius of the 1914 "Miracle Braves."

−City of Toronto Archives

A 1929 photo of the area in which the Toronto Baseball Grounds ("The Park Over The Don" or Sunlight Park) was located. Park got its name because of proximity to Sunlight Soap Works (in background).

TORONTO	AB	R	H	PO	A	E
Osterhout, rf	4	1	0	0	0	0
Alberts, rf	1	0	0	1	0	0
Morrison, cf	5	1	2	2	0	1
Faatz, 1b	4	1	1	8	0	0
Smith, 3b	4	2	2	2	2	2
Veach, p	3	3	1	0	10	0
Spill, ss	4	1	2	0	3	0
Humphries, c	4	0	0	12	1	1
Darling, lf	4	1	1	1	1	1
Macklin, 2b	4	0	1	1	1	0
Totals	37	10	10	27	18	5

Box Score of First Game
Toronto Baseball Grounds
("The Park Over The Don")
Saturday, May 22, 1886

ROCHESTER	AB	R	H	PO	A	E
Visner, lf	4	0	0	2	0	0
Kienzle, cf	4	0	0	1	0	0
Kennedy, 1b	4	1	1	9	0	1
Knight, rf	3	1	0	1	0	0
Caskins, ss	4	1	0	1	2	2
Parker, 2b	4	0	0	2	1	1
Warner, c	4	0	1	7	3	0
Whitney, 3b	3	0	1	1	3	2
Maul, p	2	0	0	0	6	1
Totals	32	3	3	24	15	7

Earned runs—Toronto 4.
Two-base hits—Smith, Spill, Faatz.
Three-base hit—Veach.
Strikes called off Veach 18, off Maul 26.
Balls called on Veach 61, Maul 62.

Passed balls 0.
Wild pitch 0.
Struck out—Torontos 5,
Rochesters 8.
Time of game—2 hours.
Umpire—Corcoran.

Baseball Place, a short, dead-end street west of Broadview Avenue, commemorates Toronto's first baseball stadium.

PROGRAMME of Band Concerts and Other Attractions:

At Hanlan's Point for the Season 1897

A two-hour Band Concert every evening and Saturday afternoon (weather permitting) by one of Toronto's celebrated Military Bands.

Grand Bicycle Races every Saturday evening by the fastest Canadian and American riders.

Eastern League Baseball

TORONTO at Home with

Springf'ld, June 12	Springf'ld, July 27	Buffalo, August 17
Springfield " 14	Springfield " 28	Buffalo " 19
Springfield " 15	Springfield " 29	Buffalo " 20
Rochester " 21	Scranton " 30	Springf'ld, Sept. 7
*Rochester " 22	Scranton " 31	Springfield " 8
Rochester " 23	Scranton Aug. 2	Springfield " 9
Syracuse " 24	Wilkesbarre " 3	Wilkesbarre " 10
Syracuse " 25	Wilkesbarre " 4	Wilkesbarre " 11
Syracuse " 26	Wilkesbarre " 5	Wilkesbarre " 13
Buffalo a m.July 1	Rochester " 6	Scranton " 14
Buffalo,p.m. " 1	Rochester " 7	Scranton " 15
Buffalo " 2	Rochester " 9	Scranton " 16
Buffalo " 3	Syracuse " 10	Providence " 17
Providence " 23	Syracuse " 11	Providence " 18
Providence " 24	Syracuse " 12	Providence " 20
Providence " 26	Buffalo, August 16	

*Two Games in afternoon at one price of admission.

Games called at 4 p.m. excepting Saturdays and Holidays, 3.30 p.m. Morning Games 10.30 a.m.

SAT., JUNE 19—Lacrosse Match—La Nationale (Montreal) vs. Tecumseh.
SAT. JULY 17—Lacrosse Match—Quebec vs. Tecumseh.
Other Lacrosse Matches being arranged
WED. AUG. 18—Toronto Police Amateur Athletic Association Games.

Roof Garden
Every Evening—Rain or Shine—at 8.15,
10c.——ADMISSION——10c.
Reserved Seats, 15c.   Children 5c. and 10c.
Change of Artists Every Week

Continuous Performances
RICH & RAMSAY
Managers

This Programme Subject to change

THE
Toronto Ferry Co.
LIMITED

TIME TABLE

For Season 1897

Steamers leave from the WEST SIDE of YONGE ST SLIP and from Brock St. Wharf.

The Company reserves the right of altering this Time Table.

BRANCH OFFICE
YONGE ST. WHARF
TEL. 2965

W. A. ESSON,
MANAGER
HANLAN'S POINT

Island Telephone, Hanlan's Point

1890-1899

A game of musical chairs and Toronto discovers an Island home

Baseball was in a turbulent mood in 1890 and Toronto would suffer as much as any baseball town before matters were resolved.

A revolt broke out involving players and owners in the National League and American Association (also a major league) and when it was over the dissidents had formed the Players' (Brotherhood) League.

Leading the revolt were Charles Comiskey and a Toronto man, Arthur Albert Irwin, known as Foxy or Cutrate. Irwin was a versatile character who at times was a photographer's model, equipment inventor and baseball author. He was a major league player for 12 years, managed four big league teams and owned a controlling interest in the Washington team during the pre-1900 era.

Irwin later managed and owned part of the Toronto team but in 1890 baseball was involved in an expensive war. Foxy and his brother John were jumping to the Brotherhood. The International League was in turmoil as cities moved from one league to another. In all this uproar, Toronto's club ceased operations July 9. It would be five years before the Torontos (they weren't yet known as the Leafs) would be back in organized ball.

The musical chairs began when Buffalo was awarded a Players' League franchise. By June Buffalo's minor league team had shuffled off to Montreal for four or five games and then went to Grand Rapids, Michigan. When Buffalo abandoned Montreal the Hamilton team quickly moved its club into the Quebec metropolis.

Meanwhile Rochester, Syracuse and Toledo bolted to the American Association, leaving the International League with six shaky franchises. Bidding for players by the three major leagues led to widespread contract jumping as salary offers skyrocketed. (Alan Eagleson couldn't be blamed for any of this mess.)

For the first time in its history the International League disbanded before the season's end. At the time Detroit and the Saginaw-Bay City Hyphens were slight percentage points ahead of Toronto, which had won 30 of its 50 games.

The 1890 Toronto team was managed by Charlie Maddock, who had been a member of the famous Maple Leafs of Guelph when it claimed the world championship. Maddock had gnarled, twisted fingers as catchers in those days didn't wear gloves. Face masks were also unheard of.

John Coleman, who also played in right field, was the team's top pitcher with an 11-4 record.

In 1890 the rules had progressed to a point where batters were out on three strikes and four balls were good for a walk. But the foul ball strike wasn't in use. It was also a truly "dead ball" era. John Grim and a shortstop named Ike tied for the team's home run leadership as each hit one on the final day of the abbreviated season.

The Players' League lasted only one season. In 1891 the American Association also folded. Toronto fans had to be satisfied with an amateur league featuring the Beavers and the

Time table and Eastern League schedule for baseball fans travelling by ferry boat to the Island in 1897.

Dauntless with the winners receiving a trophy from A. G. Spalding.

In 1891 the Buffalo Express observed: "Lovers of the game are suffering greatly in Toronto for baseball."

By 1895 Toronto was back in organized ball, replacing Erie in a league now known as the Eastern. It had changed its name when the Canadian teams withdrew.

Pittsburgh supplied most of the players in 1895 and Maddock was back as manager. He was replaced part way through the season by John Curtis Chapman, who had previously managed Detroit and four other major league teams.

The Toronto team, which had to share its playing field with amateur teams, opened at home before 1,500 fans. Cannonball Crane, the hero of 1887, lost a 2-1 decision to Scranton.

Toronto's outstanding players in 1895 were Jimmy Casey, who later played over 1,000 games and collected more than 1,100 hits in the majors, third baseman Judson Smith, who led all hitters in the league with a .373 average and 14 homers, and outfielders Fred Lake and Bunk Congalton of Guelph.

Lake amazed fans one day when he collected two doubles, a triple and homer and on another occasion when he scored six runs in a game. Years later he replaced another ex-Toronto player, Deacon Jim McGuire, as manager of the Red Sox.

The Toronto club lost a considerable sum of money in 1896 even though the total salary of the club was only $128 a day. The club switched some of its games to Albany, N.Y., but that was only a temporary move.

One of the greatest sluggers ever to wear a Toronto uniform arrived in 1896. John F. (Buck) Freeman, a wiry individual weighing less than 160 pounds, entertained fans with his seven homers and .322 average.

In 1897 and '98, when Toronto fans saw their team play in a new park at Hanlan's Point on the Island, Freeman took dead aim at the short right-field fence. He slugged 43 homers in those two seasons, leading the league both years, and hitting .357 in 1897 and .347 in 1898, tops in the Eastern League.

Buck could field as well as hit. Often he threw men out at first base on hits to right field. He went up to the majors in 1899 and

clouted an amazing 25 homers for Washington, a total exceeded only once before.

He was home run king for Boston in 1903, runnerup in '02 and '04 and once hit two triples in one inning, a major league record. He was one of Boston's hitting stars in the club's World Series triumph over Pittsburgh Pirates in 1903 and later became an umpire in the International League.

Also wearing a Toronto uniform in 1896 was Jack Dunn, who pitched and hit .242 in 27 games. Dunn later became the tyrannical, battling manager of the great Baltimore teams which won seven successive titles—1919 to 1925. He was the man who signed Babe Ruth for a $600 bonus in 1914 and developed and controlled many players who later became brilliant big league stars, among them Lefty Grove.

Dunn in 1896 was involved in a rare occurrence. Toronto dropped a tripleheader in Syracuse as Dunn lost the morning game and Herky Jerky Morton and Harry Staley were beaten in the afternoon.

The 1897 season was a pivotal year for Toronto as it boasted one of the finest minor league teams ever assembled. That's the year baseball made its debut on the Island at Hanlan's Point Stadium.

Lol Solman, the great impresario, owned a restaurant on the Island and eventually took over the Toronto Ferry Company, which purchased the baseball franchise and players from its original owners. It was an excellent way to get fans to ride Solman's ferryboats.

Solman also sponsored the lacrosse team which moved to the Island too. For 50¢ a fan could get a seat at the park and transportation. Solman, an avid sportsman, was the man who got Tim Daly started on his long career as trainer of the hockey and baseball Leafs.

Lol hired Daly as a painter to keep the stands and fences of the Island Stadium in good appearance but after watching Daly spill more paint on the ground than on the fence he figured Daly's painting was costing him more than the job was worth.

"It'll be cheaper to hire you as a trainer," said Solman.

On May 21, 1897, Toronto played its first game on the Island and lost 11-10 to Rochester before a chilled crowd. To enliven the festivi-

THE STATE OF THE INTERNATIONAL

In spite of the announcement from Detroit that the International League would not disband, the impression remains with the public that as soon as the players that are wanted elsewhere can be disposed of the affairs of the league will be wound up. The London Free Press says that is what will be done with the Tecumsehs. There was no game in Hamilton yesterday, the Hams telegraphing that the grounds were wet. The reason was that they did not want to pay the guarantee to the Torontos, as they could not draw it at the gate. A Hamilton despatch says that a renewed effort will be made to continue a team in that city at largely reduced salaries, but that can be only temporary. Detroit is ready to quit at any time, but Toronto will stick if the league goes on.

LONDON WITHDRAWS

London, July 7—The directors of the Tecumseh Baseball Club have withdrawn from the International League. The players will arrive here from Detroit in the morning, be paid off, and the club disband. This means the collapse of the league.

The Toronto Globe
July 8, 1890

Toronto's great 1897 team which upset champion Syracuse for Steinert Cup in post season playoffs: Front row (left to right) Doc Smith, Bob McHale, Jimmy Casey, manager Arthur (Foxy) Irwin, Welcome Gaston, Billy Lush and Pop Staley. Top row: Jack White, N. Norton, Cooney Snyder, Bill Dinneen, Dan McGann, Pop Williams, Wally Taylor, Buck Freeman. Staley was the great National League pitcher of the era and Casey, Dinneen, Freeman and McGann later starred in the major leagues.

Possibly first Toronto baseball program (1899) using color on cover.

Far right: Big Bill Dinneen, pitching ace for Toronto in 1897 and star of first World Series for Boston.

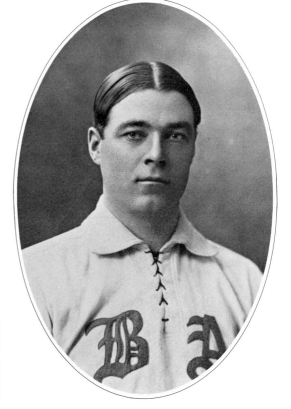

25

Jack Dunn was a Toronto pitcher in 1896 and later gained considerable fame as a manager and the man who signed Babe Ruth.

ties a band greeted players at the dock after they had paraded from the Grand Union Hotel.

At one point 12 ferries were shuffling fans back and forth to the Island to see Big Bill Dinneen.

Dinneen won 21, including 17 out of 18 during one span. Toronto also had an awesome batting attack. The big hitters were Freeman in right, who ripped Rochester pitching for a homer and four doubles one afternoon, catcher Doc Casey, first baseman Dan McGann, who hit a league record 22 triples and batted .354 and Billy Lush, a .319 hitter.

McGann, Freeman and Casey enjoyed prolific careers in the majors. But it was Dinneen who gained the highest accolades. Four times he won more than 20 games. He and the famed Cy Young were the 1903 pitching stars for Boston in the first World Series, which resulted when the Red Sox challenged the National League's leaders, the Pittsburgh Pirates.

Dinneen shut out the Pirates twice in winning three of his four decisions. Before he retired to a long career as an umpire, Dinneen tossed a no-hitter against the Chicago White Sox, hurled 37 consecutive complete games and went the entire 1904 season (337 innings) without relief assistance.

Managed by Foxy Irwin, the 1897 Toronto team lost 20 of its first 25 games and then just failed to catch the Syracuse Stars for the pennant. A Syracuse brewer put up a trophy, the Steinert Cup, to settle which club was the better. Toronto went into Syracuse, won three in a row and settled the issue in the fourth game at home.

Irwin's 1898 team finished third, with Kirtley Baker and Welcome Gaston each winning 17 games. A .333 hitter for Toronto was 40-year-old Dan Brouthers, later referred to as the "Babe Ruth of the 1880s and 1890s." He was the mightiest slugger of the period; five times he won major league batting titles and hit over .300 fourteen times. He had a lifetime average of .349 and was elected to the Hall of Fame in 1945.

The 1899 season brought a new manager, Wally Taylor, and a fourth place finish. Jim (Foxy) Bannon won league hitting honors with .341 and Romer Grey hit seven homers.

As for the Eastern League it was still in a state of chaos. Toronto and Buffalo were both offered franchises in Ban Johnson's Western League, forerunner of the American League. Buffalo accepted. Wilkes-Barre folded.

Rochester was the bad-luck team of the era. After its one year in the majors in 1890 Rochester returned to the minors for two years. But fire destroyed Culver Field late in 1892. The Hop Bitters (they were also known as the Brownies, Jingoes, Bronchos, Hustlers and Tribe before Red Wings) were out of ball until 1895.

Two years later Rochester's new stadium also burned down and the franchise was shifted to Montreal while a new grandstand was built. When the 1898 season rolled around Montreal refused to relinquish the franchise so Rochester had to buy Scranton's.

Business was so bad that Rochester finished the season in Ottawa. But this time they maintained control of their franchise. With Wilkes-Barre and Buffalo out in 1899 the league acquired the Worcester Saucemakers and Hartford.

The decade ended with pitchers heaving from 60 feet, 6 inches (the present distance) and abolishment of the pitcher's box with hurlers obliged to place a foot on the slab.

Foul balls, however, were not strikes unless they were caught by the catcher. Bunts that rolled foul were now strikes.

Dan Brouthers, the "Babe Ruth of the 1880s and 1890s" hit .333 for Toronto in 1898.

Hugh Duffy, one of the
National League's great
hitters before managing a
good 1920 Toronto team.

An 1897 game at Hanlan's Point. The lone umpire stood back of the pitcher, who didn't have a mound to throw from. Home team batted first in this game.

1900-1909

Barrow, Kelley, J. J. and three parks

The first decade of the century brought incredible changes and personalities to Toronto baseball life.

One man, Edward Grant Barrow, later went on to create the mightiest empire baseball has ever known, the New York Yankees. Another, Joseph James Kelley, had been regarded as the "king pin" of the famed Orioles of the John McGraw era.

Both would guide Toronto to pennants and later be enshrined at Cooperstown, N.Y., in the Hall of Fame. A third individual, a local boy, was James Johnstone McCaffery, the friendly owner of the Bay Tree Hotel, who would team up with another showman, Lol Solman, to save ball in Toronto.

League franchises continued to shift. Buffalo returned in 1901, replacing Springfield. The following year Jersey City and Newark took over from Syracuse and Hartford. McGraw's Baltimore team was booted out of the American League, returned to the minors and took Montreal's franchise. The Royals in June inherited the Worcester franchise.

For the next 10 years the league was stable.

The Toronto team played in three different parks during the decade and changed ownership twice.

The period also witnessed the arrival of some glorious players – Bullet Jack Thoney, an outfielder, swift and challenging at the plate and on the bases; Bill Carrigan, superb as a catcher and later as a manager, winning two World Series; Dick (Baldy) Rudolph, who

won 120 games in Toronto before getting a chance to be the pitching star of the 1914 World Series; and Nick Altrock, a crafty southpaw.

Altrock, used as a pinch-hitter by Washington as a stunt when he was 57, gained as much fame as a comedian after a distinguished pitching career with the White Sox.

Altrock hooked up with the legendary Mordecai (Three-Fingered) Brown in the all-Chicago 1906 World Series, beating Brown 2-1 and then losing 1-0.

However, the big man to appear in Toronto in the 1900s was Barrow, who later was to assemble the Yankee dynasty of the 1920s, '30s and '40s and who converted Babe Ruth from a pitcher into a slugging home run hero while managing the Red Sox in 1918.

Barrow was a man of many talents when he arrived in Toronto in 1900. He bought Arthur (Foxy) Irwin's quarter share of the club and took over as manager. Barrow had been a journalist, clerk and manager of a hotel in Pittsburgh and had once owned a soap factory with his brother Frank. But people in Pittsburgh didn't care for his soap in those days and the business failed.

Barrow was also a noted pugilist, a boxing instructor and fight promoter in Philadelphia before forming the Atlantic League and operating the Paterson, N.J., team. One of his discoveries was the Flying Dutchman, Peter (Honus) Wagner, the greatest shortstop in the history of baseball. Barrow sold him to Louisville of the National League.

Flames destroy Island's second stadium in August, 1909. Team moved to Fraser Avenue's Diamond Park until new park was built for 1910 season.

34

A summer holiday crowd boards the Blue Bell for a game on the Island.

Following the 1900 season, which was highlighted by Charley Carr's hitting (six singles one day against Syracuse), 52 Toronto businessmen formed a company to buy the club back from the Toronto Ferry Company.

The group was headed by Ed Mack the tailor, Jess Applegath the hatter and Thomas Soole the printer. Purchase price was between $6,000 and $10,000.

They made a deal for transportation with the Toronto Street Railway and moved the club from the Island to a park on Fraser Avenue, behind the site where Mercer Reformatory once stood, south of King Street and east of Dufferin. Barrow was to receive $1,500 with a bonus of $300 if the team finished first or second.

The shrewd Barrow won his bonus. The club finished second behind the pitching of Pop Williams and Altrock, a great money pitcher who loved the tough games.

The 1901 opening ceremonies at the new field, later called Diamond Park, were colorful to say the least. The season opened May 10 against Worcester Saucemakers with a 25¢ admission to the grandstand and 50¢ for reserved seats.

The procession to the park was typical of the gala parades which preceded each home opener. A total of 13 tally-hos (horse drawn carriages) carried the players, who sat up high so that thousands of onlookers could get a good look at not only their heroes in uniform, but also team officials, shareholders, sportswriters and equipment.

Opening day and horse drawn tally-hos paraded through streets with players and Newark officials in 1909.

With the Queen's Own Rifles leading the way the procession moved along Simcoe, King, Yonge and Queen Streets, stopping in front of the then new City Hall for introductions and speeches.

Worcester won the game 6-5 and afterwards the Toronto Globe writer observed: "How could the locals win after passing two funerals on the way to the park?"

Jimmy Bannon and Frank Bonner each hit .340 to lead the club's attack. Bonner also hit 10 homers but the captain and second baseman was attacked viciously in the press when he jumped to Cleveland in 1902.

"According to manager Ed Barrow, Bonner is the champion contract-breaker of the world. Bonner made many friends by his brilliant playing last year, but his lack of principle and moral rectitude, as evidenced since then, has caused him to sink to a low place in the estimation of those who know him."

Purchased by Toronto for $600, Bonner had a chance to almost double his salary ($1,400 to $2,400) by going with either Chicago or Cleveland. Bonner wrote Barrow and said if Barrow would send him $100 he would sign with Chicago, who had promised to reimburse Toronto for its original $600 outlay. Barrow sent the $100 but Bonner signed with Cleveland.

Barrow's pennant-winning 1902 team was blessed with a trio of outstanding pitchers – Louie Bruce, a marvellous Indian athlete who regularly hit over .300 and played shortstop when not pitching; Herb (Button) Briggs and Jimmy Gardner.

Gardner won both ends of a doubleheader on the final day of the season to give Toronto the pennant by a half-game over Buffalo. Bruce compiled a .900 pitching percentage with an 18-2 record, a mark which stood until 1937 when Atley Donald of Newark beat it with 19-2.

Gardner was 19-4 and Briggs 20-8 that pennant year. Bill Massey, Duke Esper, Jack White, Lewis Carr, Eddie Miller, Jack Toft and Yencer Wiedensaul were also key members of the team. Barrow went up to the Tigers in 1903. Gardner took over as manager and finished third.

Ol' Foxy Irwin returned in 1904 but gave way to Dick Harley before the season was over

as the club fell back to sixth. Then came eighth place finishes with Harley and White in 1905 and again with Barrow, who had lost his magic, in 1906.

During this period business faltered. Bondholders foreclosed their mortgage on the club. Pittsburgh was interested in acquiring the team but pub owner J.J. McCaffery purchased it for $21,800 and cleared all debts. In weeks a new stock company was formed with capital of $25,000. J.J. Seitz was the new president with McCaffery and Solman in the "background". A year later McCaffery took over personally, and was to become one of the most respected men in baseball.

McCaffery remained as head of the club until his death in 1922 at his home on Toronto Island.

During the early McCaffery years the Toronto ball program advertised his Bay Tree Hotel at Bay and Adelaide as the place "for the finest of wet goods on dry days." Players 75 years ago eagerly offered their names for endorsements.

One ad said, "A great pair – Jimmy Bannon and Griffith's Menthol Liniment – They're Both The Best."

In the lean years Toronto fans had to be content with the pitching of Briggs (26-8 and league leader in strikeouts, 205), Clarence Currie, Cy Falkenberg and Jim McGinley, who won 100 games in six years. At the plate the versatile Bruce hit .356 and won 12 games. White twice led in hitting and Jim Murray topped league home-run hitters with nine in 1905. Thoney won the first of his two batting titles in 1906, slamming out 32 doubles and 173 hits.

Then came Kelley, in 1907 – Joseph James Kelley of earlier Oriole fame.

In the 1890s there had not been a more feared or respected club in baseball than the Baltimore Orioles of Ned Hanlon and the feisty John McGraw – a brawling collection of talented players.

They were innovators, the authors of "inside baseball." They perfected the bunt, the squeeze play, the hit and run and the "Baltimore Chop." Win at almost any cost was their motto. Soon the opposition was copying their strategies for advancing the runner.

It was a club that included at least five Hall

Crafty Nick Altrock, a great pitcher and comedian. Altrock was 16-game winner.

Edward G. Barrow led Toronto to a 1902 pennant before creating New York Yankee empire.

Joseph James Kelley, king pin of the Orioles in McGraw era, was pennant-winning manager.

Myron Grimshaw, first baseman and league batting champ with .309 for Toronto in 1909.

Fred Mitchell pitched and caught. Tossed a no-hitter, won $50 for riding donkey.

This may be the pennant winning 1902 team at Diamond Park on Fraser Avenue. The team included pitchers Button Briggs, Louie Bruce and Jimmy Gardner, who won both ends of a doubleheader on the final day of the season to give Toronto the title, catcher Jack Toft, first baseman Bill Massey, shortstop Lewis Carr, second baseman Jimmy Miller, outfielders Jack White, John Golden and Yencer Wiedensaul.

The serious looking group is Toronto's pennant winning team of 1907 which won the Junior World Series. The men in bowlers at left are owners Lol Solman and James J. McCaffery. Top row (left to right): Elmer Moffitt, Larry Hesterfer, Jerry Hurley, Torren, Jim McGinley, Middle row: Fred Mitchell, Bill Carrigan, Jack Thoney, Fred Applegate, manager Joe Kelley with daughter on lap, Bill Phyle, Yencer Wiedensaul and Larry Schlafly. Bottom row: Woods, Dick Rudolph, Jimmy Frick, Jim Flood.

Jersey City, N.J., June 30—(Special) — . The frequent breaches of discipline recently in the Eastern League have aroused the ire of President Powers, and he has resorted to prompt measures to suppress all further rowdyism in contests here and in other cities on the circuit.

This morning Mr. Powers fined Catcher Brown of the Torontos $10 and suspended him for three days. "Sandow" Mertes was fined $25 for the trouble he and Brown started last Friday in the games between Toronto and Jersey City.

For the mix-up in yesterday's game between Baltimore and Jersey City, President Powers suspended Pitcher Dessau indefinitely. Dessau attacked Umpire Moran. Manager Jack Dunn is fined $25 for his part in the fracas. For his failure to report the trouble with the Baltimore players to the headquarters of the league President Powers announced the release of Umpire Moran, to take effect immediately.

The resignation of Umpire Sullivan has also been accepted. His successor has not yet been named.

President Powers says he is determined to eliminate rowdy ball-playing from the Eastern League, and if fines and suspensions fail to suppress the violations of the rules he will resort to the permanent black list. Pat intends to make trouble for every player who makes trouble for him.

The Toronto Globe
July 1, 1908

of Famers. Slugging Dan Brouthers was at first, the scrappy Hugh Jennings at short, Wee Willie ("Hit 'em where they ain't") Keeler in right, the combative McGraw at third, Wizard Hoffer and Joe McGinnity on the mound and Joseph James Kelley in the outfield.

Kelley was a powerful hitter (.391, .371, .370 and .390 in one four-year span) with a strong arm and tremendous spirit and magnetism. One year he stole 90 bases and when he left the Orioles he took over as captain of the National League champion Brooklyn Superbas for two years.

He went on to manage the Cincinnati Reds, a team whose lineup included Miller Huggins, Gabby Street, Cy Seymour, Sam (Wahoo) Crawford, Noodles Hahn and the forgotten man in the Tinkers-to-Evers-to-Chance infield of the Cubs, Harry Steinfeldt.

It was this same Kelley who arrived in Toronto in 1907 to take over an eighth place club. Fans immediately fell in love with the big Irishman. The team soon was known as the Kelleyites as they swept to the pennant behind the pitching of McGinley (22-10), the promising newcomer, Rudolph (13-8), Elmer Moffit and Larry Hesterfer.

Carrigan was the catcher, a .319 hitter who later went to the Red Sox as playing manager and beat the Phillies and Dodgers in the World Series. Kelley (.322) was in centre. The hard-luck Thoney won another batting title (.320) that year but suffered a bad shoulder injury while taunting a pitcher as he danced off first base. He stole 76 bases and scored 93 runs.

Thoney had been called the "next Ty Cobb" because of his slashing, daring style of playing but the injury crippled his throwing arm, and career.

The club, which also included Fred Mitchell, a pitcher-catcher, third baseman Bill Phyle, second baseman Larry Schlafly, shortstop Jimmy Frick and first baseman Jack Flynn, easily whipped Columbus of the American Association in the Junior World Series, winning in five games and sharing a sum of $692.92.

Toronto's joy was short-lived, however, as the Boston Beaneaters drafted Kelley, who protested that he would not go as he didn't want to leave Toronto, but did.

In 1908 Toronto returned to Island Stadium with another Kelley in charge, Mike Kelley who wouldn't last the season. Schlafly took over. Phyle, who led the team in hitting and was tops in the league with his 16 homers, smashed a two-run shot on opening day as Toronto edged Jersey City 7-6.

For the first time since 1885 a Toronto pitcher tossed a no-hitter. Mitchell, the converted catcher, beat Montreal 2-0. An even better pitching performance was turned in by Moffitt, who allowed a first inning single then held Buffalo without a hit in winning 1-0 in 14 innings.

Like so many Toronto players, Mitchell wound up in the majors as a manager. He faced an old mate, Barrow, in the 1918 Series as Ruth and the Red Sox downed Mitchell's Chicago Cubs in six games.

Before leaving Toronto, Mitchell entertained fans and won a $50 bet from Solman when he rode a donkey that had escaped from a fire at the Island's zoo. Mitchell circled the bases and then sold the donkey to a Queen Street butcher for another $50.

The old wooden Island Stadium burned to the ground during the season of 1909. Toronto finished the season at Diamond Park on Fraser Avenue. That was the last year on the mainland until 1926. A new concrete Island stadium was being built by Solman, McCaffery and associates.

In the 1909 season Joe Kelley returned from Boston and had a club which hit only 17 homers. Rudolph with 23 wins and McGinley with 22 were again the club's leading pitchers while Myron Grimshaw led the league in hitting with .309.

First baseman Ben Houser slugged six homers while Kelley at 38 still managed to play centre with style as he made only one error all season.

An opening day crowd at Diamond Park and Jack Thoney is on his way to his second batting title. Swift and daring on the base paths, an injury prevented him from achieving stardom in majors.

Outstanding as a catcher in Toronto, Bill Carrigan achieved greater fame in the majors. He managed Boston Red Sox to back-to-back World Series triumphs.

Dick (Baldy) Rudolph pitched a no-hitter and won 120 games before reaching majors. He was pitching star of Boston's "Miracle Braves" in 1914 World Series.

A panoramic shot of opening day in 1908 as baseball returns to the Island. The championship pennant (far right) flutters in breeze. Note the bowler hats and the well-dressed women standing behind the outfielders. Tips of the masts of sailboats, a diving board and the roller coaster can be seen.

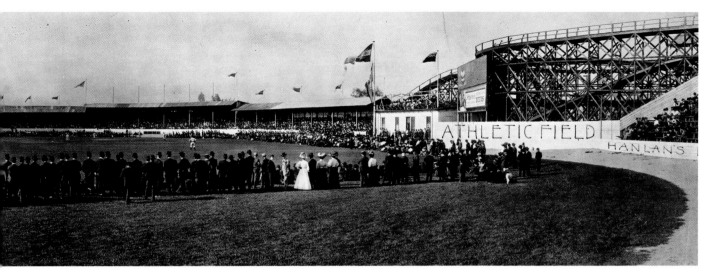

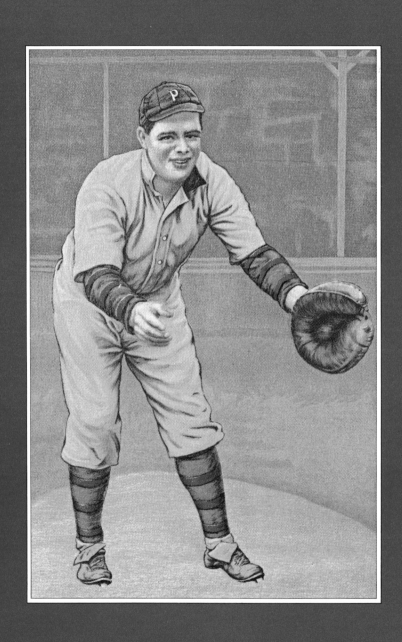

1910-1919

Three pennants and a precocious teen-ager, Babe Ruth

The gaudiest era in Toronto's baseball history began in 1910 when the first exuberant but chilly fans flocked from the mainland to the new 18,000 seat concrete stadium at Hanlan's Point.

The Island's first wooden stadium had burned down in 1903 when the Toronto club was playing at Diamond Park. The second went up in flames in 1909. The new one, called Maple Leaf Park, was to be the home of three championship teams in the next decade – Toronto winning pennants in 1912, 1917 and 1918.

A lanky 19-year-old, Babe Ruth, hit his first professional home run at that stadium while tossing a one-hit 9-0 shutout for the Providence Grays. Another two of baseball's most prolific hitters, Napoleon (Larry) Lajoie, and Wee Willie Keeler, spent their final seasons in the game delighting fans who made the trip across the bay on ferryboats Bluebell, Trillium, and Mayflower.

Lajoie had been the great Cleveland hitter while Keeler had starred with the old Orioles and the early Yankee teams.

Two other notable characters familiar at Hanlan's Point were one of baseball's great spitball pitchers, Urban Shocker, and Dapper Dan or Howlin' Dan Howley. Shocker in 1916 established two International League pitching records for consecutive runless innings and fewest earned runs allowed which still stand. Howley won a pennant in his first season and went on to lead Toronto to more wins than any other manager in the club's long history.

The era was also highlighted by Joseph James Kelley's second pennant in 1912 and Lajoie's memorable triumph in 1917, the only time in his 23-year career that the elegant big Frenchman played on a championship team.

The decade was further enlivened by the towering homers big Timmy Jordan lofted over the right field barrier and into Toronto Bay along with the slashing hitting of Mike Slattery, Fred (King) Lear, Benny Meyer, Maurice Rath, Bob Fisher, and Eddie Onslow.

On the mound, Dick (Baldy) Rudolph reeled off 18, 23, and 25-win seasons before moving up to the big leagues. Rudolph, like Shocker, pitched extra inning no-hitters in the era. Rudolph pitched hitless ball until the 11th, when a Montreal player singled. In the 12th, however, Joe Delahanty singled for Toronto, moved to second on Bill O'Hara's bunt and scored on Slattery's drive to centre for a 1-0 victory.

Twice John McGraw of the Giants drafted Rudolph but sent him back to Toronto, saying he was too small to pitch in the majors.

A popular story was that Rudolph failed to make the Giants because he won everybody else's money playing poker, disrupting the morale of the club. Anyway, he hadn't stuck.

Back in Toronto, Rudolph was earning the league limit, $450 a month, but wasn't happy. After losing a tough 1-0 decision to Newark one day, he said he was through with baseball unless Toronto sold him to a big league club. Preferably Boston.

Team president J. J. McCaffery acted quickly

London's Moony Gibson, clever, durable Pittsburgh catcher, managed Toronto in 1919; then Pirates and Chicago Cubs.

and did sell him to the Braves. Rudolph, who had won 120 games, more than any other Toronto pitcher before or since, showed McGraw he could play in the big leagues. He won 122 and compiled an enviable major league mark of 26 shutouts and a lifetime ERA of 2.66.

His biggest moment came a year after he left the Leafs.

Rudolph was a member of George Stalling's "Miracle Braves", the club that went from last place on July 6 to a pennant, winning by more than 10 games over McGraw's Giants. That was one pleasant revenge. There was more to come. Until 1914 no club had ever swept a World Series in four games. The Braves accomplished the feat in whipping the world champion Philadelphia A's of Connie Mack. Rudolph beat Chief Bender in the first game on a five-hitter (the only A's run was unearned) and outpitched Bob Shawkey and Herb Pennock in the fourth and deciding game, scoring the winning run in the 3-1 contest.

He was 27-10 that year and following the Series, Joe Vila of the New York Sun, having listened a lot to McGraw, said to Rudolph, "I see you have become quite a pitcher."

Rudolph replied: "I always was."

Ellis Johnson was pitching for Toronto on September 5, 1914, when the rookie Providence pitcher, Babe Ruth, drilled a three-run shot – the first pro homer of his great career – over the fence in right. Only hit off Ruth was catcher Billy Kelly's single in the fifth.

On Monday morning, The Globe baseball writer wrote, "Ruth, the tall, left-handed pitching sensation of the Providence team held the Kelley's to one hit. This youngster is not yet old enough to vote but he can heave that old pill and the Boston Americans made no mistake when they bought him from Baltimore."

Ruth led all International League pitchers with 22 wins that year.

By coincidence, Ruth's first two major league homers in 1915 came off Chief Jack Warhop, who became a Toronto pitcher in 1917 and 1918 when the club won back-to-back pennants. Warhop was an underhand pitcher.

Toronto had a lot of good pitchers in those years. Besides Rudolph there was Harry Thompson, who won 25 to lead the league in 1917, Fred (Bugs) Hersche and Bunn Hearn.

Others included Wilbert Hubbell who had a 1.91 ERA mark and won 17 games in 1919, Adolfo Luque, a great major league star in later years, Clint Rogge, Bull Wagner, Reb McTigue, Kid Mueller, Jim McGinley, Johnny Lush and Hal Justin.

But Shocker's efforts in 1916 would never be topped in Toronto.

That year he pitched an 11-inning no-hitter against Rochester, set an IL mark of 54 consecutive runless innings and posted the lowest ERA in any minor league, an amazing 1.31. He also won 15 of his 18 starts. His pay that season was $250 a month.

When the major leagues passed a rule in 1920 banning the spitball, Shocker and Rudolph were among the 17 pitchers who were allowed to keep using the pitch until they retired. Last of the wet-ball bunch to retire was Burleigh Grimes, who later managed the Leafs.

Nap Lajoie was 41 when he arrived in Toronto to manage and play "a little" in 1917. He had pounded out more than 3,200 hits during his big league career as a second and first baseman with the Indians, Athletics and Phillies and was considered by oldtimers as baseball's greatest second baseman.

Describing his style, a New York Sun writer wrote: "Every pose was a picture, yet there was no striving on Lajoie's part for artistic effects. His gracefulness was innate, a part of this eye-filling D'Artagnan of the diamond. Ruskin referred to architecture as 'frozen music.' Lajoie's batting and fielding might with equal propriety be termed 'living poetry'."

A less flamboyant Cleveland writer observed: "Old Nap Lajoie was the only man I ever saw who could chew scrap tobacco in such a way as to give a jaunty refinement to a habit vulgar and untidy in so many others."

Lajoie was handsome, big and dark, with bold features and arresting eyes. He wore his cap cocked on the side of his head, which was covered with thick, dark, wavy hair. The uniform roll collar of the day he wore casually, partly turned up, to make an attractive frame for his face.

With a flourish, he'd draw a line in the dust alongside home plate with the business end of his bat as a prelude to facing the pitcher. The

Timmy Jordan was Brooklyn's home run king before belting drives into Toronto bay.

Handsome, graceful Larry Lajoie won many bat titles but one pennant–1917 Leafs.

Providence pitcher Babe Ruth hit only minor league homer against Toronto on Island.

Wee Willie Keeler, Orioles' "Hit 'em where they ain't" batter, at 39 was a 1911 Leaf.

Adolfo (Pride of Havana) Luque, a 15-game winner before great career with Reds.

Urban Shocker, famed spitball pitcher in majors, set marks for Toronto which still stand.

Aerial view of Hanlan's Point in 1915, which shows rebuilt amusement park and the modern, 18,000 seat Maple Leaf Park.

bat spoke eloquently. Sixteen times he hit over .300, including an American League record of .422 in 1901.

In Toronto he played first base and assaulted minor league pitching to lead the league with a club record .380 average. Among his 221 hits were 39 doubles, four triples and five homers. Toronto had to sweep a doubleheader on the final day to edge Providence but in the Junior World Series against Indianapolis the Leafs lost 4-1 with spitballer Abner Gould getting the lone Toronto win on a one-hitter.

Wee Willie Keeler was 39 when he joined his old Oriole playing buddy, Kelley, in Toronto in 1911. Keeler, whose 44 game major league hitting streak held up until Joe DiMaggio came along, just missed getting 3,000 hits in his major league career before coming to Toronto. He hit .278 for Toronto on a club that won 94 games but finished third.

But, to go back a little: Opening day ceremonies for the new ball park on the Island in 1910 were curtailed somewhat because King Edward VII died the day before the opener, but 13,000 showed up on a cold, blustery May 10 day to see Albert Shaw's homer lead Toronto to a 4-3 win over Baltimore.

The Leafs of that day wore white uniforms, black trimmings and a white "T" on the sleeves as well as an embroidered green silk leaf.

Slattery, the first baseman, led the league in fielding and hitting and Shaw topped home run sluggers with 11. The following year, 1911, Slattery hit .342 but lost the league batting title by a percentage point. Jordan's 20 homers took the home run title. Before joining Leafs Jordan twice won home run titles in Brooklyn.

Jordan, noted for his head first slides, was the big man in Kelley's second pennant winning year in 1912, clouting 19 homers and hitting .312. One day at the Island he slammed

50

two drives into the bay, hit two singles and knocked in eight runs.

Bill Bradley, for years one of the finest third basemen in the majors, and Amby McConnell were the good infielders of this era. In 1913, Hearn pitched a record 20-inning 0-0 tie against Jersey City.

For a while the IL flourished with its new president, Ed Barrow, appointed in 1911. But in 1914 two wars developed – one in Europe and the other in baseball. The Federal League was organized by a group of wealthy men who decided the time was right for a third major league. The IL's strong cities, Baltimore, Buffalo and Newark, were invaded earning the league the title of "The Belgium of Baseball".

The Toronto territory for the Federal League was reportedly handed over to a Brooklyn baker, Robert Ward. It was a ruse, however. Ward intended to take the franchise to Brooklyn to advertise his "Tip Top" bread. Anyway, the Federal League never did come to Toronto.

The Federal League's invasion caused several franchises to shift elsewhere. Baltimore's went to Richmond and Newark to Harrisburg and then back again. Richmond later refused to give up its franchise so Baltimore bought Jersey City's. Hit hard, the IL reorganized. Barrow quit when his salary was cut in half.

Richmond, Providence and Montreal dropped out in favor of Jersey City, Binghamton and Syracuse, which eventually shifted to Hamilton for a year before going to Reading.

The Federal League lasted two years but it did attract many big stars with its huge pay cheques. Joe Tinker, Three Fingered Brown, Canada's Russ Ford, Benny Kauff, Hal Chase, Edd Roush, Ed Ruelbach, Eddie Plank, Chief Bender, and ex-Leafs Cy Falkenberg, Hearn, Rogge, Shaw, Meyer, Carr and Ernie Herbert all jumped their clubs.

Meanwhile back in the stricken IL, Toronto struggled along despite poor attendance and operating losses. In 1915 Bill (Derby Day) Clymer, who ranked with Jack Dunn as the most astute manager in the minors, took over from Kelley. His judicious trades and clever handling landed the team in third place.

Joe Birmingham, a veteran major league manager and Russell (Lena) Blackburne, a

First baseman Jack Slattery, batting and fielding champ.

character who would manage Toronto on four occasions, shared duties in 1916.

Blackburne, who loved baiting umpires, kicked up such a fuss after Leafs lost twice to the Rochester Hustlers that umpire Chester said he wouldn't allow Leafs on the field the next day until Blackburne paid his $20 fine. Blackburne handed over twenty $1 bills the next afternoon.

Then came the Lajoie and Howley pennant teams of 1917 and 1918, each winning the title on the final day. Howley's team did it with a dramatic flourish as it won by a slim two percentage points over Binghamton.

On the final day of the 1918 season both the Leafs and Bingos were scheduled to play a doubleheader. A pennant hinged on Toronto winning both ends of morning-afternoon games against Buffalo while Binghamton split against Baltimore.

The suspense on the Island grew as both Leafs and Bingos won their first game. But when Baltimore's 2-1 win in the second game was posted on the scoreboard the Toronto players and fans knew they had a chance.

The game went into extra innings and Buffalo scored a run in the 10th. But Toronto came back with a run to tie the game at 4-4 and won the pennant in the 12th on King Lear's bases loaded hit to deep centre.

The clutch-hitting Lear drove in four of Leafs' five runs, including the tieing run in the 10th, stole three bases and made 20 putouts at first. He led the team in hitting and homers that year and was its key performer along with pitcher Fred (Bugs) Hersche, a 21-game winner.

The seventh manager in six years, George (Moony) Gibson of London, Ont., took over in 1919. One of the most durable catchers in the history of the NL, Gibson lasted only one year before going up to manage the Pirates and Cubs. Gibson's Leafs won 93 games but finished second to Baltimore, which did not lose another title until 1926.

Getting to the Island presented several problems for fans as they first had to dodge trains at the Yonge St. crossing.

It's opening day at the new Hanlan's Point stadium and the
two teams stroll arm-to-arm across field after introductions.

The league champion Torontos of 1912. Front row (left to right): Benny Meyer, manager Joe Kelley, president J. J. McCaffery, Peaches Graham, Amby McConnell, Kid Mueller, Dick Rudolph, Tim Jordan, Ed Fitzpatrick, Eddie Holly, Al Shaw, Harry Bemis.

Back row: Bert Maxwell, Elmer Stricklett, Bill O'Hara, Johnny Lush, Charles Isaacs, business manager Rube Bernstein, captain Bill Bradley, Jack Dalton, Harry Curtis and Louis Drucke. In front is trainer Tim Daly.

1920-1929

It was the Roaring '20s, a raucous and exciting period in baseball.

Babe Ruth was slugging the livelier ball farther than any hitter in history. The Chicago "Black Sox" scandal was headline news. Three National League players were barred, without publicity, for throwing games.

Life in Toronto was almost as exotic. Fans warmly welcomed veteran Benny Kauff, known as the Ty Cobb of the Feds when he played in the old Federal League.

Kauff was a hard-hitting outfielder "loaned" to the Leafs by John McGraw of the Giants. A few years earlier Kauff was a bon vivant on the order of Joe Namath. In his first season with the Indianapolis Hoosiers of the short-lived Federal League, he hit .370, stole 75 bases and led in doubles, runs and hits and lived in a style befitting a champ, complete with diamond rings and silk underwear.

Traded to the Brooklyn Tip Tops in 1915, Kauff again led the league in hitting and stolen bases. When the league folded the Giants paid a record $35,000 for Kauff. Twice he hit over .300 in New York before inexplicably being sent to Toronto in 1920.

A few months earlier Kauff had accused teammates Hal Chase and Heinie Zimmerman of offering him a bribe to throw a game. Apparently there was hard evidence since McGraw dropped the talented pair from the team in the middle of a close pennant race.

Prince Hal, one of baseball's great fielding first basemen but a notorious gambler, former batting champion Heinie Zimmerman and

Chicago Cubs' Lee Magee were quietly blacklisted from organized baseball.

Another story was that Kauff had been mixed up with a car-lifting mob in New York, making Toronto a good place to visit while things cooled. Leafs had a great team in 1920, won 108 games and played .701 ball but still finished second to Jack Dunn's Baltimore Orioles.

Kauff, along with Eddie Onslow, Frank O'Rourke, Vern Spencer, Lena Blackburne, Jim Riley, Andy Anderson and Mike Devine, all hit over .300 that year. But Kauff was the leader, batting .343 and 12 homers. He was as good an outfielder as Leafs ever had during their Island playing days.

Unfortunately Kauff's reputation – and the auto story – followed him to rival parks. He would be greeted by fans armed with automobile horns. One day in Jersey City the groundskeeper had left the steamroller in deep left. A fan bellowed, "Hide that machine quick, here comes Kauff."

Before another season rolled around baseball's new commissioner, Judge Kenesaw Mountain Landis, barred Kauff for life. Some observers felt Landis acted harshly as a jury acquitted Kauff on a charge of receiving stolen goods.

The Leafs of the '20s averaged 93 wins a season yet won only one pennant, in 1926. They finally caught the Orioles in the pennant race. If you could pick out one magical year in the club's 79-year history, that would be it: 1926.

John McGraw of the Giants inexplicably loaned batting star Benny Kauff to Toronto in 1920. The flashy Kauff led Leafs in hitting and homers but was barred from baseball the following year.

59

For years Leafs had played on the Island. Crowds were often large and lusty. There were no floodlights, of course. Brokers, clerks, merchants and the general public contrived somehow to scurry to the docks, catch the ferry and get to the game by 3 o'clock.

Wednesdays, when many stores closed, were usually good days; but Saturdays and holidays were even better.

The crowd would arrive at the stadium in tidal waves as each boat unloaded. Fans would gallop to the park and rush to the best available seats. Then there was a lull until the next ferry released its quota of fans.

By late 1925 there were suggestions that the Island wasn't a choice location. The 1920 club had drawn 207,570 but attendance had been declining even though Leafs had exciting, winning teams.

So Leafs moved. Club president Lol Solman sold his ferryboat fleet and Island holdings and moved the Leafs into a new, ultra-sophisticated stadium built in five months at a cost of $750,000 at the foot of Bathurst Street. It was the most modern structure in the minors, a 20,000-seat stadium built on seven acres of reclaimed land owned by the Toronto Harbor Commission.

Toronto fans, justly proud, dubbed the stadium the "Fleet Street Flats" and reporters turned to knocking the Island park that had been just fine in previous years.

A Toronto Globe reporter wrote critically of the Island era, saying, "No longer will the fans have to travel across the treacherous railroad tracks and take an 'ocean voyage' that all disliked. The famous 'bullpen' has passed along."

Another said, "The ferry trip and the daily dodging stunt across the railroad tracks discouraged fans and attendance fell off. The 'regulars' suffered on occasions when there were over 12,000 fans and some had to remain on the Island for an hour after the game had finished before they could make ferry connections."

Another boasted, "We'll show the world the kind of ball town Toronto is. When we look around the mammoth stadium we are inclined to speculate on the question of Toronto for the major leagues. Who knows? It's up to the fans."

This was the type of enthusiasm which greeted manager Dapper Dan Howley's team when they returned from their season-opening, highly successful road trip. More than 1,000 fans turned out to watch the team work out in the new park.

Rain caused a day's postponement of the opener and it was frigid (33 degrees) and drizzling on April 29 when more than 14,000 listened to the Queen's Own Rifles play the anthem.

Fireworks exploded and parachutes, with Union Jacks attached, unfolded and floated to the field. The first pitch was thrown by Mayor Robert Foster to "batter" Tommy Church, a former long-time mayor of the city.

As for the game, the last place Reading Keystones, who eventually finished 75 games back of the champion Leafs, attacked Toronto's pitching ace, Walter (Lefty) Stewart and reliefer Joe Maley for a 5-0 lead.

In the last of the ninth the crowd was lingering in the aisleways with two out as Toronto suddenly broke loose against curveballer Jim Marquis. Four runs scored. Mickey Heath tied it and sent the game into extra innings with a clutch hit.

Owen Carroll, who won 21 games that year, set the Keystones down in the 10th before Leafs won in the most exciting way possible – Del Capes executed a perfect squeeze bunt play at the plate and Herman Layne raced in from third with the winning run.

Lead-off man and centrefielder for Leafs that opening day was Babe Dye, former Toronto sandlotter who also possessed one of the hardest shots in the National Hockey League. He was a right-winger with the Toronto St. Pat's.

Dye, who had two hits in the game, was traded shortly afterwards to Baltimore. Another great hockey player with the '26 team was Lionel Conacher, but his name doesn't appear in league statistics.

One fan of that club recalled, "I don't think Conacher cared much for baseball. I believe he played in only one game, the last of the season and he struck out on three pitches."

Only person to find fault with the new park was baseball commissioner Judge Landis.

Looking at the white lettering on a red background which spelled "Maple Leaf Sta-

Eddie Onslow, the slick fielding first baseman, is only Toronto hitter with more than 1,000 hits. He managed Leafs for one season – 1922.

1922 Score Book

Owen Carroll, 21-game winner.

Joe Kelly, top hitter 1924-25.

Claude Satterfield–no-hitter.

Rip Collins won 17 in 1928.

Playing manager Steve O'Neill.

Myles Thomas, 28-8 in 1925.

Carl Hubbell, a future great.

John Prudhomme–two no-hitters.

Home run champ Al (Red) Wingo.

What a rally! What a game! No fiction-story teller could imagine a more thrilling setting than that which the battling Howleyites staged for themselves in the ninth inning here yesterday afternoon, when, in the drizzling rain, they scored five runs to tie the count with Reading at 5 to 5, and to send fourteen thousand loyal fans into one of the wildest demonstrations of joy that the new stadium will ever see. For eight consecutive innings Jim Marquis, ace of the Reading pitching staff, mowed down the locals with neatness and despatch, and when they entered the final frame there were few in the vast throng who conceded the Leafs a chance to win the game. But win it they did, the deciding run being shoved over in the tenth frame.

The great rally came like a shot from the blue. Carlyle, first man up in the ninth, pounded out a single and Layne duplicated the feat. Miller, however, grounded out, but the fans got a chance to cheer a moment later when Capes hit a sacrifice fly to Whitman, scoring Carlyle.

Howley Drives Them

Two out in the ninth and four runs down. It seemed an impossible feat to overcome that lead, but Dan Howley stood out on the coaching line at third base and urged his players to stick to their guns. Howley was the man behind when the pinch arrived. He knew what to do, and his well trained athletes had the ability to follow his instructions to the letter.

The Toronto Globe
April 30, 1926

dium," Landis said, "I don't often abuse the absolute authority reposed in me, but that won't do. As High Commissioner of Baseball I command that this beautiful place be called Solman Field, and that's that!"

Solman, involved with the club since the pre-1900s, rejected the idea.

In 1926 more than 222,000 fans, a record which stood until 1948, watched with delight as Leafs finally snapped Baltimore's seven-year monopoly on first place. The man guiding Leafs, Howley, spent the next six years managing St. Louis and Cincinnati in recognition of his skillful managerial ability.

Howley, who had taken over Leafs in 1923, had a young, hard-hitting club that led the league with an amazing team average of .308. On defense it was exceptional, although Orioles edged Leafs by less than a percentage point for league fielding honors.

Leafs possessed great speed and each member of its outfield, Cleo Carlyle, Layne, Tilly Walker, Frank Gilhooley and Capes, hit .300.

But the main source of Toronto's attack came from its infield. Billy Mullen at third led the team in hitting with .357. Shortstop Otis Miller knocked in 120 runs and batted .345. Minor (Mickey) Heath at first had 115 RBIs and hit .335. Carl Schmehl, Otis Lawry and Andy Harrington divided up the second base duties.

Leafs had the clever Steve O'Neill and Lena Styles behind the plate. O'Neill, Gilhooley and Heath won defensive honors at their positions.

The pitching staff was almost as potent at bat as on the mound. Claude Satterfield hit .353 and Jesse (Slow Motion) Doyle .370. Both were often used as pinch-hitters.

Backing Stewart and Carroll were Doyle and Jim Faulkner, a pair of 15-game winners, and relievers Maley, Red Fisher, Vic Sorrell and a young pitcher who wasn't allowed at the time to use the pitch which eventually put him into the Hall of Fame – Carl (Meal Ticket) Hubbell.

Leafs then were a farm team of the Detroit Tigers. Hubbell was under orders not to fool around with a pitch he liked to throw – the screwball, a reverse curve which broke down and to the left, away from right-handed hitters.

To pitch it, the strain on the elbow is considerable. Tigers felt Hubbell would ruin his arm. With Toronto, Carl was only 7-7.

Within a couple of years, he was traded out of the Tigers' farm system to Beaumont of the Texas League. There he perfected his screwball.

Rediscovered by the New York Giants, Hubbell went up to the majors for 15 years during which he won 253 games and twice was voted the league's most valuable player.

He gained fame in 1934 when he fanned five of the American League's greatest hitters in the All-Star game. Among his pitching feats were winning 24 games in a row over two seasons (16 in a row one season) and 46 consecutive runless innings.

Hubbell didn't pitch, however, in the 1926 Junior World Series as Leafs raced to an unprecedented 5-0 sweep over the Louisville Colonels. Doyle and Stewart each tossed a shutout as the Toronto pitching staff held the Colonels to six runs.

Leafs graduated one man after another to the majors. None ever rivalled the batting and fielding exploits of the Mechanical Man – Charlie Gehringer.

He was with the 1925 Leafs, a club that hit .305 and won 99 games. It was obvious the 22-year-old belonged in the majors after his year of "seasoning" on the Island.

All he did was score 128 runs, hit safely 206 times for a .325 average, wallop 38 doubles, nine triples and 25 homers, two with the bases loaded, and knock in 108 runs. Defensively he was as good, leading all second sackers with a .966 average.

Gehringer played baseball in an effortless style and used a minimum of words. His Detroit manager Mickey Cochrane once said, "He says 'hello' opening day, 'goodbye' closing day and, in between, hits .350."

Over 17 seasons Gehringer batted .321 and was selected to the all-star team five times as well as winning MVP honors in 1937 when he won the batting championship.

Gehringer entered the Hall of Fame in 1949.

Toronto produced another AL batting champion in the 1920s in Dale (Big Boy) Alexander, a tall, lumbering first baseman who dominated International League pitching for two years but especially when he won the triple crown in 1928.

Also nicknamed Moose, Alexander clubbed a record 49 doubles, 236 hits and 144 RBIs. He led all batters with a .380 average (previously attained only by Lajoie) along with 11 triples and 31 homers.

Elevated to the Tigers, Alexander had little difficulty adjusting to big league pitching, with years of .343, .326 and .325. But he also led the league in errors for first baseman.

He played 23 games in 1932 before the Tigers sent him to Boston and Fenway Park. There he fell in love with the towering but close fence in left. Alexander batted a league high .367 with the Red Sox but, because of his hopeless fielding, within two years was out of the majors.

Kauff, Gehringer, Miller, Mullen, Heath and Alexander were not the only outstanding hitters of the '20s for the Leafs. Go back to 1920 and Frank O'Rourke, who ranks as probably the best shortstop to ever play for Toronto. He was a Hamilton boy who at 18 injured his arm playing with Brooklyn, an injury which always troubled him although O'Rourke played more than 1,100 games in the majors.

He was superb with the glove and had astounding speed. Three times he scored from second on fly balls. Twice during the 1920 season he slammed out six hits in a game. Against Rochester he had two homers, a double and three singles; and attacked Reading pitching for three doubles and three singles.

First baseman Eddie Onslow, who holds the record for most hits by a Toronto batter with 1,111, was a consistent .300 hitter and also had six hits in a game. His big day in 1920 was against Buffalo when he had a homer and five singles.

His fielding was just as competent. Onslow should have stuck to playing, for when he managed Leafs in 1922 they finished out of the first division for the only time in the decade.

Joe Kelly and Absalom Holbrook (Red) Wingo were also remarkable hitters in Toronto uniforms. Kelly hit for a high average and slugged the long ball. Wingo was just as impressive as he earned promotion to the Tigers when he hit 34 homers and followed up

the following season with a .352 average.

Wingo, however, had the misfortune of having to crack a Detroit outfield which included Ty Cobb, Harry Heilmann and Heinie Manush, who were elected to the Hall of Fame, and Bob Fothergill.

Toronto had an unusual collection of outstanding pitchers in the decade. Hugh Duffy, the Hall of Famer who hit .438 for the Boston Nationals in 1894, managed the 1920 club which included Pat Shea (27-7), Rosy Ryan (19-9), Lore Bader (19-9), Maurice Craft (8-0) and Bill Snyder (8-1).

The Orioles had to win 25 in a row in the final month to edge this Leaf club. This was also the year the schedule maker put different clubs into Toronto on one day and Leafs split a doubleheader on August 27 against Jersey City and Syracuse.

Laughin' Larry Doyle, the great Giant second baseman, and Lena Blackburne, an all-star third baseman, managed Leafs in 1921. That year Jesse Altenburg led the team in hitting with .346 but cost Leafs a game when he refused to leave the field in Baltimore after being evicted for disputing a called third strike.

One feature of the 1924 season was that Claude Satterfield pitched a no-hitter, 1-0 over Jersey City. Also Lefty Stewart made his debut with the team and led the league by completing 31 of his 35 starts (24 wins). Stewart won 63 games in three seasons with Leafs and 100 more in the majors.

He was just as effective in 1925, winning 21 games and edging teammate Myles Thomas, a 28-game winner, for the league ERA title – 2.513 to 2.515. That year Leafs won 19 in a row but as usual finished second to the Orioles.

Also making his debut with the club in 1924 was an assistant to the colorful Tim Daly, a skinny 14-year-old batboy – Bill (Smitty) Smith. He may have made history that year as the only batboy to be ejected from a game.

It happened during one of the morning-afternoon doubleheaders. Leafs were losing and didn't appreciate the umpiring of Carpenter. When Carpenter asked for a fresh supply of balls, Leaf catcher Mike Vincent gave Smitty careful instructions on how to hand the ump the balls. As Carpenter reached for them Smitty dropped them on the ground.

Fielding wasn't Dale Alexander's forte. Won Triple Crown for batting in 1928.

Dan Howley managed most wins.

20-game winner Guy Cantrell.

Pat Shea was 27-7 in 1920.

Gehringer: Leafs' best at 2nd.

Hugh Duffy won 108; ended 2nd.

Stadium builder Lol Solman.

The greatest Toronto team? This is the 1926 team which won 109 games and swept Louisville 5-0 in the Junior World Series after stopping Baltimore's string of pennants at seven. Left to right: Frank Gilhooley, Otis Lawry, Bill Mullen, Andy Harrington, Steve O'Neill, Herman Layne, Carl Schmehl, Claude Satterfield, Walter Stewart, Tilly Walker, Carl Hubbell, Jim Faulkner, road secretary

A packed stadium and politicians greeted the Leafs on opening day, 1928: (From left) Mayor Samuel McBride, master of ceremonies Victor Gianelli, Premier Howard Ferguson, Controller Joseph Gibbons, Controller Bert Wemp, Controller William Robbins, Bill Phillips, Erwin Sexton, Lena Styles, Clarence Fisher, Stainton Lucas, Claude Satterfield, manager Bill O'Hara, Harry Davis, Warren

The umpire, after kicking the teen-ager out of the game, had to pick them up. The Leaf players roared. Smitty went to the dressing room in tears. Daly, the "kindly old trainer", suggested that Smitty apologize, which he did. Then Carpenter allowed Smitty to resume his duties.

Except for a couple of war years, Smitty was with the club until the end in 1967.

No-hitters? John (Augie) Prudhomme did it twice at the new stadium. On both occasions he received stout support as he beat Reading 14-0 in 1927 and Jersey City 5-0 in '28.

Joe Rabbitt, aptly named since he stole 46 bases, Ralph Shinners, Bill Sweeney, John Stone, Bucky Burke and playing-manager

Bill O'Hara, vice-president James Dunn, manager Dan Howley, president Lol Solman, Joe Maley, Lionel Conacher, Lena Styles, Cleo Carlyle, Owen Carroll, Jesse Doyle, Vic Sorrell, Mickey Heath, Bill Skiff, Otis Miller, trainer Tim Daly, bat boy Bill Smith and mascot Fred (Murph) Blandford.

Cote, Les Burke, Clayton Sheedy, Bill Webb, Merwin Jacobson, George Rensa, Dale Alexander (who led league in hitting, RBIs and homers), Steve Martin, coach Fred Burchell, John Prudhomme, who pitched his second no-hitter as a Leaf, Fred Bedore, Walmsley, Sam Gibson, Fraser and Don Hankins.

O'Neill powered a good 1929 team.

Rabbitt had 16 homers, including three one afternoon against Baltimore, while Shinners led the team's hitters with .337. The club's only 20-game winner was rookie Guy Cantrell.

One of the sad moments of this otherwise happy period came with the death in 1922 of James J. McCaffery, the tavern owner who along with Solman saved the club in the early 1900s and who led the club with imagination and great determination through some bad years.

Nothing was too good for Toronto fans, or baseball, in his opinion. He even financed the Syracuse franchise during the First World War when it was on the verge of collapse.

Beautiful shade trees and picnic benches greeted fans who travelled to Hanlan's Point for games at stadium built in 1910.

Police direct traffic on a cold, wet opening day of April 29, 1926, at new stadium. Many fans parked in fields or along road instead of paying 15¢ for parking adjacent to stadium.

Patches of snow are visible as workmen using cranes and horse-drawn wagons are busy erecting Toronto's ultra modern stadium on seven acres of reclaimed land owned by the Toronto Harbor Commission.

It took five months to build and cost $750,000 in 1926 for the finest park in the minor leagues—Maple Leaf Stadium. Note the bleacher seats back of the warning track in left field.

PHOTO BY THE T. EATON Co. LTD

The 1926 International
League champions and
Junior World Series winners
on a cold opening day at the
new Maple Leaf Stadium.

Box Score of First Game
Maple Leaf Stadium
April 29, 1926

READING	AB	R	H	PO	A	E
Pitt, rf	5	2	4	2	0	0
Krehmeyer, ss	5	0	2	2	3	0
Jacobs, lf	5	1	3	5	0	0
Whitman, cf	5	2	2	1	0	0
Keesey, 1b	5	0	1	11	1	0
Sigafoos, 2b	5	0	2	2	2	0
Wright, 3b	5	0	1	0	1	0
Lynn, c	5	0	0	4	1	0
Marquis, p	4	0	1	1	5	0
Totals	44	5	16	28	13	0

TORONTO	AB	R	H	PO	A	E
Dye, cf	5	0	2	2	0	0
Heath, 1b	5	0	3	9	1	0
Carlyle, rf	4	1	1	1	0	0
Layne, lf	4	2	1	4	1	0
Miller, ss	4	0	0	3	2	0
Capes, 3b	4	0	2	3	2	0
Schmehl, 2b	3	0	0	3	1	0
bHarrington, 2b	1	1	1	0	0	0
O'Neill, c	4	1	1	5	0	0
Stewart, p	2	0	0	0	4	1
Maley, p	0	0	0	0	1	0
Carroll, p	0	0	0	0	0	0
a-Styles	1	0	0	0	0	0
c-Satterfield	1	1	1	0	0	0
Totals	38	6	12	30	12	1

a—Struck out for Stewart in 8th.
b—Singled for Schmehl in 9th.
c—Singled for Maley in 9th.

		R	H	E
READING	100 002 101 0	5	16	0
TORONTO	000 000 005 1	6	12	1

Error—Stewart.
Double plays—Toronto (Layne to
Schmehl). 2b—Wright.
Runs batted in—Capes (2), Harring-
ton, Satterfield, Dye, Heath; (Reading
RBIs unavailable).
Hits off—Stewart, 13 in eight innings;
off Maley, three in one inning.
Bases on balls—Off Stewart 1, Carroll
1, Marquis 2.
Struck out—By Stewart 4, Carroll 1,
Marquis 3.
Winning pitcher, Carroll.
Sacrifice hits—Krehmeyer, Miller,
Capes.
Stolen base—Pitt.
Wild pitch—Marquis.
Left on bases—Reading 12, Toronto 8.
Time—2:15.
Umpires—Carpenter and James.
Attendance—12,781 (paid).

1930–1939

Depression turned on the lights as well as Ike.

The 1930s brought the great economic depression, The Second World War and the irrepressible Isaac Morgan (Ike) Boone.

Night baseball came to Maple Leaf Stadium and Lawrence (Lol) Solman, the dynamic individual responsible for the building of the park, died.

It was a decade of poor crowds and mediocre baseball teams. One lost a record 113 games. Only 49,963 paid to watch that sorrowful 1932 squad. Attendance during the entire decade totalled only 1,124,569.

But the 1930s weren't completely bleak.

You could watch characters such as Hot Potato Hamlin, Peanuts Pezzullo, Steamer Lucas, Bots Nekola, Hoot Gibson, Skabotch Samuels, Gunner Cantrell and Izzy Goldstein on the mound. And on the base paths were Stinky Davis, Lu Blue, Porky Howell, Poosh 'Em Up Tony Lazzeri, Twinkletoes Selkirk, Ollie Sax, Flea Clifton, Tubby Reiber and Oreb Hubbell.

It was also an era when Leroy Herrmann and Bill Weir, a pair of southpaws, tossed no-hitters and the surprising Leafs of Ike Boone won the Shag Shaughnessy playoffs (another innovation of the '30s) before going nine games in losing the Junior World Series to Columbus in 1934.

The depressed economy of the period hurt all of the minor leagues, struggling to stay in business. In Toronto the death in 1931 of the club's long time benefactor, Solman, worsened matters.

Early that year Solman lost control of the stadium to the Toronto Harbor Commission because he was $60,000 in arrears with taxes and rent.

The popular showman, involved with the club since its first days on the Island in 1897, died a few months later. He had often been described as "the Shubert of Canada" because of his involvement in theatres, shows and amusement parks. At the season's opener players from both teams formed a cross on the diamond from the plate to the mound and a crowd of 11,629 sang "Abide With Me".

Following Solman's death George Oakley took command of the club. His son Clifford inherited the club in 1935 but was forced to sell after the 1936 season. The new group was bankrolled by philanthropist Percy Gardiner and Donald G. Ross.

For the Leafs the 1930s started slowly and then got worse. Only exception was Boone's good 1934 team and it could draw only 136,301. But despite the fact Leafs finished in the first division only twice in the decade they had many outstanding players.

Bob Elliott and Frank McCormick later won MVP awards in the National League. Dixie Walker won a NL batting title and returned in the 1950s to lead Leafs to a pennant.

Billy Rogell and Marv Owen played for Toronto before joining ex-Leaf Charlie Gehringer in the infield of the champion Detroit Tigers of 1934-35. George McQuinn twice batted over .300 for Leafs and went on to make it big in the majors.

Parking space was even a problem in 1932 as fans parked their Model Ts fender to fender in parking lots just to the east of Maple Leaf Stadium.

Johnny Allen, to become a star with the Yankees, Indians and Dodgers; Rip Sewell, Luke Hamlin and Phil (Babe) Marchildon were ones with the good young arms.

Allen won 21 games (17 with Leafs) in 1931. He was a temperamental but cocky right-hander. One afternoon against Rochester he sent Leafs' clubhouse boy over to the visitor's dressing room with $50 and orders to get the Red Wings to put up $50 for a "friendly" wager on the outcome of the game.

The Wings "covered" Allen's ante with $1, $2 and $5 bills and the Leaf hurler promptly went out and tossed a shutout. A year later Allen with the Yankees in a pennant winning year, snapped off 11 wins in a row.

Hamlin was the only Leafs' pitcher to win 20 or more in the '30s (21-13 in 1933). He followed with a 20-win year for Brooklyn in 1939.

Playing alongside the young potential stars were men who could no longer make it in the majors or fellows who would never make it.

Joe (Moon) Harris at 39 was still good enough to slug three pinch-hit homers and lead all Toronto batters in hitting, RBIs and homers in 1930. An outfielder, Harris had been one of the hitting stars of the 1925 World Series for Washington when he smashed three homers, two doubles and hit .440.

Heinie Manush, who hit .330 and had over 2,500 hits in a distinguished big league career which earned him a spot in the Hall of Fame, arrived in Toronto at the tail end of his playing days but hit .310 in 81 games in 1938.

Also winding up in Toronto were Lazzeri, the great Yankee slugger who managed Toronto's eighth place team in 1939, and Steve O'Neill, manager of the 1929-31 teams. O'Neill went on to become an outstanding manager with Cleveland, Boston Red Sox, Philadelphia Phillies and Detroit; his Tigers winning the 1945 World Series over the Cubs.

The 1930s also involved the heroics and antics of dapper but incisive John Berly, a great relief pitcher who appeared in 52 games for a last place 1939 team; the swift, hard-hitting Joe Rabbitt; Luzerne (Lu) Blue, whose wife was a Ziegfield Follies beauty; Tommy (Reb) Oliver, who occupied centrefield with grace; Joe Morrissey, who had six singles in a game

against Syracuse; Joey Gantenbein, a slick shortstop and catcher Frank Reiber, who each hit two grand slam homers.

Others worthy of mention were Jack Burns, a fancy fielding first baseman who managed poor Toronto teams; smooth Lee Handley at third; Nolen Richardson, another superb infielder, and outfielders Ivey Shiver, John (Rocky) Rothrock, Clayton Sheedy, Ted Petoskey, Mayo Smith, Bobby Porter, the Toronto Beaches hardrock and Wes Schulmerich.

Schulmerich, a long ball hitter in 1935, loved to taunt pitchers by retreating off second base. Instead of taking a lead towards third he'd dance back towards first base in an effort to draw a throw.

His antics were finally curtailed when the league brought in a rule forbidding this type of stunt.

Red Smith, a Notre Dame great before his brilliant National Football League career, was a catcher for Leafs and Ken Strong, who made football's Hall of Fame as a New York Giants' back, led all Leafs hitters in 1931 with a .340 average. He also hit three homers and fanned three times against Buffalo one afternoon.

Along with Allen, Sewell, Hamlin and Marchildon, pitchers of note included Joe Sullivan, tops in the International League with 18 wins in 1938; Guy Cantrell, best for three years; Gene Schott, Whitey Hilcher, Ralph Birkofer, Jim Pattison, Silas (Si) Johnson, Jake Mooty and Joe Mulligan.

Herrmann had to hold Newark hitless for 10 innings on May 2, 1936, before first baseman Leo Scarsella counted Leafs' only run in the bottom of the 10th. Weir received much more support in an 8-0 no-hitter on May 16, 1939.

Toronto's slugger of the '30s, Ike Boone, won a box of cigars for hitting a homer the night the lights were first turned on at the stadium in 1934. He'd been a football star with the University of Alabama and became the minor league's greatest hitter of his time.

The Mob? No, it is Toronto officials, players and newsmen heading south for spring training. Top (from left) is Bill Smith, Dick Mitchell, Bob Porter, Art Upper, Al Leary and Gord Walker. Front row: Nat Turofsky, Tim Daly, Ben Milner, Don Ross, Fred Crawford, Dick Mansell, Art Leman and Bert Perry.

He won batting titles wherever he played; three times over .400. He wasn't noted for hitting them out of the park because he belted line drives. But in 1929 at Mission in the Pacific Coast League he slugged 55 homers.

Boone could also hit major league pitching. He had a .319 average during his many visits to the big leagues. But he was rather slow footed, a liability on defence. Today he could earn $100,000 a year as a designated hitter.

He was 36 when his tour finally landed him in Toronto in 1933. Boone had a 32-game hitting streak (a modern team record) that year, batted .357 and led the team in RBIs and homers. But Ike was just warming up for his remarkable 1934 campaign.

Following a dispute over salary between Oakley and manager Dan Howley, Boone was handed the manager's job. Ike proceeded to rip pitching for a league leading mark of .372, earn the MVP award and lead Leafs to a berth in the Junior World Series after upsetting pennant winning Newark and Rochester in the playoffs.

The American Association's representatives, Columbus, got a jump on Boone's Leafs in Toronto when its ace, Bear Tracks Geer, won the opener 7-1. It was a good series and was tied 4-4 before Columbus won the deciding ninth game at home.

Although night baseball had been played experimentally as early as 1880, it didn't become a reality until 1930 when two teams in the Western Association and Buffalo (July 3 v. Montreal) installed lights.

Minor league operators were unanimous that night baseball would be their salvation but Toronto held off installing lights until 1934. On June 28 that year floodlight baseball groped its way into Toronto. Leafs officials announced they had "the best lighting system in Canada." Leaf players weren't so sure after Rochester beat them 8-2 and complained about shadows and unlit areas.

Not entirely confident about their new toy, and reluctant to start until complete darkness set in, officials announced that the game would begin at approximately 9:45 p.m. To keep the fans entertained they brought in famed baseball comedian Nick Altrock, who had gained fame in 1901 at Diamond Park by winning 16 games for Leafs before a lengthy major league career with the White Sox and Senators.

Altrock and a local comedian, Hap Watson, put on a show that lasted until after 10 o'clock. When it took an hour to play the first three innings the 16,000 fans became impatient and began booing. Another delay occurred in the seventh when peanut peddlers became involved in a brawl.

It was after 1 a.m. when Rochester's Cowboy Winford retired the last Leaf batter, making Boots Hollingsworth the losing pitcher. Toronto's only runs came on Boone's two-run homer. As Boone crossed home the fan who had promised him a box of cigars jumped up and shoved a $5 bill through the screen and said "buy yourself the best box of cigars you can get." In 1934 those would be good cigars.

Leafs staggered out of the '30s in last place with a weak hitting outfit. Only Boone in 1934 and O'Neill in 1930 were able to guide Toronto into the first division. Lena Blackburne, Tom Daly, Burns and Lazzeri failed.

Howley in 1933 and '37 was unable to apply the magic he worked with the great 1918 and 1926 teams. After managing the Browns and Reds, Howley returned to Toronto with the hope of becoming a part-owner of the team. When he was denied this privilege Howley quit after one year.

He rejoined the team in 1937 when Gardiner and Ross took control but Toronto finished a distant seventh.

Despite Leafs' lack of success on the field and at the box office, seven men who either played or managed the club – Boone, Hamlin, O'Neill, Selkirk, Dixie Walker, Howley and Berly (he rarely journeyed by train without his six-shooter under the pillow of his berth) – were later elected to the International League Hall of Fame.

As the 1939 season neared an end Hitler was marching into Poland. In the next few years baseball lost many of its top players to other uniforms.

Brooklyn manager Burleigh Grimes (left) with two of his 1938 coaches—Babe Ruth and Leo Durocher. Grimes later managed Leafs to a pennant.

Top right: Opening day 1937 with Toronto owner Percy Gardiner, Mrs. Verna Howley and manager Dan Howley.

Public address announcements would boom through the stadium over The Globe's six foot megaphone by Ernie Ross. "Ladee-e-s an' gem'n! Battree-e-e-s for today'll be..."

Slugging Ike Boone, greatest hitter in minor leagues, led Toronto into Junior World Series in 1934 when he hit .372.

Far right: Lanky Joe Mulligan dwarfs Frank Madura, left, and Dick Henry at Toronto's Avon Park, Florida, training base.

**Playing manager Tom Daly
shared duties in 1932 with...**

...Russell (Lena) Blackburne, who also
managed in 1941, 1921 and 1916.

The new park on Fleet Street attracted industry, fans and traffic jams. Inset: the old park (top right background) where Babe Ruth hit his only minor league homer and new stadium in early 1930s.

Temperamental but cocky
Johnny Allen was brilliant in 1931.

Luzerne (Lu) Blue, one of
Toronto's many top first basemen.

Luke (Hot Potato) Hamlin
was a 21-game winner in 1933.

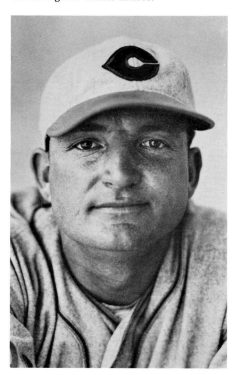

Outstanding relief pitcher and
IL Hall of Famer–John Berly.

Slugging Bob Elliott, great
with Leafs and MVP in majors.

Southpaw Leroy Herrmann
tossed 10-inning no-hitter in 1936.

Poosh 'Em Up Tony Lazzeri
managed bad Toronto ball clubs.

George (Twinkletoes) Selkirk
a Leaf before replacing Ruth.

Rip Sewell wasn't throwing his
famed Blooper Pitch in 1932.

George McQuinn was outstanding
with bat and glove at first.

Heinie Manush, one of game's
top hitters, hit .311 as Leaf.

Ken Strong hit three homers
in one game and .340 in 1931.

Bobby Porter, the Toronto Beaches hardrock, receives standing ovation from almost 20,000 Coronation Day fans in 1937 after hitting three-run homer. Greeting him are Ted Petoskey (16) and Mayo Smith (4).

PETER G. CAMPBELL
PRESIDENT AND GENERAL MANAGER   J. M. MACINTOSH K.C.
VICE-PRESIDENT   ARTHUR H. LEMAN
TREASURER   MISS A. M. HARWOOD
SECRETARY   HARRY A. DAVIS JR.
MANAGER

Toronto Maple Leaf Baseball Club Limited

OPERATING

Toronto Baseball Club

INTERNATIONAL LEAGUE

C O P Y

TORONTO,
CANADA

Lieut.Col. F. E. Anderson,
O.C. - No. 6 Ordnance Depot,
R.C.O.C.,
Willow Park, HALIFAX, Nova Scotia.

Dear Col. Anderson:

       You have in your unit Corporal William
Smith, B 1028.

       This soldier has worked himself up from
a bat boy to the position of head trainer of the Toronto Maple
Leaf Baseball Club in the International League. We are naturally
holding his position open for him and we would appreciate it very
much if there is a chance of his obtaining his release from the
Army by March 1st, as we leave for our spring training camp shortly
after that date.

       I would like to say this in favour of the
Maple Leaf Baseball Club: During the war years there have been
over a quarter of a million troops allowed into the Maple Leaf
Stadium as guests of the Maple Leaf Baseball Club free of charge
in the regular seats for every game. We have given thousands of
dollars to different local regiments and have co-operated in
every way with all the Services.

       Anything you can do towards securing his
release for us, will be greatly appreciated.

       Yours very truly,

Signed: PETER G. CAMPBELL
Peter G. Campbell:H   President

1940·1949

Help Wanted: Baseball Players

Ralph Kiner played briefly for Toronto in the 1940s but then so did Marvin Felderman, Alva Javery, Benjamin Steiner, Byron Laforest and Alphonse Mazur.

This was characteristic of the decade, an era in which all baseball was diluted by a shortage of manpower for five years because of the Second World War.

Good young players were either rushed up to the major leagues or drafted into the military service. Players who normally would have been shunted to the minors had their careers lengthened because they were too old to fight a war or were rated 4-F and not eligible for the U.S. draft.

Those the Army, Navy, Air Force and the major leagues couldn't use wound up in the minors. Desperate for players during the war, Leaf president Peter Campbell took to inserting ads in the Sporting News. They worked. He acquired pitchers Al Jarlett, Luther Knerr and Harry Jordan for an $80 help wanted ad.

Jarlett led the team in 1945 with an 18-9 record. Knerr posted a 2.96 ERA and was later sold to Connie Mack's Athletics for $15,000.

Managers for most of this period had to be miracle makers with some of the retreads and untried bodies who put on baseball uniforms. Life in the minors was tough enough anyway. It was worse in a town which didn't have Sunday baseball.

Leafs often played Saturday doubleheaders at home and then headed for Sunday games on the road, standing all the way on crowded wartime trains, returning home late at night.

One U.S. writer, assessing baseball's wartime prospects in Canada, thought "interest will be greater than ever with folks of the Dominion seeking diversion from serious affairs." He was partially correct. Attendance at Montreal's Delorimier Stadium increased each year during the war (and soared in 1946 when Jackie Robinson arrived).

In Toronto the opposite was the case. Crowds dipped to 67,123 in 1940 and 57,815 the following year. But eighth place finishes both years were not exactly a grabber, either.

Also, these figures only included the paying customers. Leaf management gave passes to more than 250,000 men and women in the services during the war years. If you were in uniform, you were in–free.

By the end of the '40s interest in baseball was in a resurgent mood as a pair of second division teams drew record crowds. In 1948 fans totalled 291,977 and in '49 Del Bissonette's fifth place team attracted more than 350,000, a record that would be broken several times during the reign of Jack Kent Cooke in the Fabulous '50s.

Although the decade spawned some desperate Leaf teams it did produce Toronto's eighth pennant winner in 1943. Guiding that club was Ol' Stubblebeard – Burleigh Grimes, one of baseball's great spitball pitchers. Five times he won more than 20 games in a season while pitching himself into the Hall of Fame for the Dodgers and Pirates.

Off to a quick start in 1943 when they won six of their first nine games before opening at

A good trainer was almost as valuable as a .300 hitter or 20-game winner during the war-time period. This letter to Corp. William Smith's commanding officer from team president Peter Campbell is explanatory.

home, the Leafs were never in trouble. They finished 9½ games ahead of Newark with a won-lost of 95-57, best Toronto record since Dan Howley's championship team of 1926.

It was a veteran club. Luke (Hot Potato) Hamlin was back, winning 21 games (he'd won 21 for the 1933 Leafs) and posting an ERA of 1.96. First baseman Harry Davis, who started his career with Leafs in 1929, led the team in hitting and RBIs.

For Hamlin, who always pitched with a big red handkerchief dangling from his hip pocket, it was the beginning of another career. He remained with Leafs until the end of the '48 season and retired with a 91-58 won-lost record.

Only two other pitchers in Leaf history, Dick (Baldy) Rudolph and Jim McGinley, won more games than Hamlin, who got his nickname when New York sports columnist Jimmy Connor said he "jiggled the ball like it was a hot potato."

Nick (Jumbo) Strincevich worked harder than any pitcher on that team. In winning 15 games, many in relief, he hurled 233 innings. The Serb also discovered more ways to lose winning games than any other pitcher.

Other important members of the pitching staff included Dick Conger, who pitched 18 innings of a 21-inning game against Baltimore; Tom Ananicz, who had a seven-inning no-hitter against Buffalo late in the season; Jarlett, Harry Shuman, Jim Hopper, Joe Sullivan and Red Kress.

Maurice (Bomber) Van Robays, Lee (Jeep) Handley, Herb (Workhorse) Crompton, a slow-moving catcher who rolled into a triple play that season, Jim Ripple, Frank Colman, the London, Ont., slugger, Jimmy Tyack, Lee Gamble, Al Rubeling and Frankie Zak were other key members of that pennant team.

A kid named Kiner was with them for 41 games and hit only two homers and .236 before the U.S. Navy signed him. Kiner did much better in the majors. He made the Hall of Fame as he slugged more than 50 homers a season, twice. Seven times he either led or tied for the HR lead in the National League with the Pirates. He finished with 369 home runs.

In the 1943 Governor's Cup playoffs Leafs dusted Montreal in four but lost in six to Syracuse.

You didn't have to read the newspapers or listen to the radio to realize a war was on. Toronto's baseball programs carried patriotic messages and suggestions on conserving energy by turning lights off while attending night games. Fans were urged to save sugar, "get an extra inning out of your tires", to send cigarettes to the troops overseas and buy war saving certificates and victory bonds regularly as "victory can only be won by the united efforts of all our people." Heroism and gallantry were portrayed throughout the scorebooks.

Handlebar Hank was the symbol of the baseball club's diamond jubilee.

Ol' Luke Hamlin returned in 1943 and again won 21 games.

Lefty Carl Fischer, brilliant at times but 0-17 in 1941.

The Pride of Ingersoll, Oscar Judd, won 14 games in 1948.

Ralph Kiner hit two homers for Toronto and 369 in majors.

Burleigh Grimes in 1943 won Leafs' first pennant in 17 years.

Toronto sportswriters, Trent Frayne, left, and Gord Walker visit ex-Leaf pitchers at Philadelphia's West Palm Beach training grounds. From left: Toronto's Dick Fowler, only Canadian to hurl no-hitter in majors, Frayne, Joe Coleman, Walker and Phil (Babe) Marchildon of Penetanguishene.

The crowds loved home run slugger Ed Sanicki. Hit 33 in '49.

The '40s had its share of exciting players, dramatic afternoons, record performances and characters.

The good players who'd later make it to the majors included Jim Konstanty. This great relief ace of the 1950 Phillies was the NL's most valuable player that year and lost a heart-breaking 1-0 game to the Yankees in the opening game of the World Series.

Other majors-bound Leafs were outfielders Johnny Wyrostek and Jimmy Russell, Philadelphia Whiz Kids Puddin' Head Jones, Stan Lopata, Mike Goliat, Jocko Thompson, Steve Ridzik, Emory (Bubba) Church and Putsy Caballero; pitchers Phil Marchildon, Strincevich, Dick Fowler, Joe Coleman and Bill McCahan.

A good Canadian product, Ingersoll's Oscar Judd, pitched a 7-0 no-hitter against Syracuse in 1948. Al Porto held Newark hitless in 1949 in a 5-0 seven inning contest.

Toronto native Goody Rosen returned home in 1947 to play for Leafs after hitting .326 for the Dodgers in 1945 and making the NL All-star team.

Home run hitters also brought fans to the park. Ed Sanicki set a stadium mark of 33 in 1949 and Bill Glynn hit more than 20 the same season. The previous year Sanicki and Hank Biasatti each hit 21.

Catchers Gene Desautels and Lopata tied the club mark for most RBIs in a single game. Each produced eight runs on separate occasions. Other record performances went to Chet Laabs, who had a homer, double and four singles against his former Buffalo Bison teammates, and Harry Davis, who drew 160 walks.

The characters included Old Folks Arntzen; Chief Vallie Eaves, who showed up at 8 a.m. at the stadium in a drunken condition and asked manager Lena Blackburne to let him celebrate his birthday on the mound; Tommy Fine, a pitcher who attempted to slug manager Elmer Yoter over the head with a bat after being lifted for a pinch-hitter and southpaw Carl Fischer.

Fischer was a curly-haired, happy-go-lucky guy with a great pitching talent. He was 13-11 and 10-12 with a pair of last place Leaf teams and then compiled a 0-17 mark in 1941. Fischer and Blackburne had a squabble over a broken slot machine during spring training that year and Fischer, who took a dislike to Lena,

suddenly lost his "stuff" and performed accordingly.

Senator Salter Hayden, team president in 1940 and '41, tells of a player he once scolded for not hustling to first base on easy fly balls or grounders.

Senator Hayden called him into his office when the fans started booing.

"He explained to me that the 36 holes of golf he played every day tired him out," said Senator Hayden.

The '40s also produced one of the wildest opening day games in the history of the club. The dramatic contest occurred in 1942 as Toronto trailed Jersey City 9-4 in the ninth. Until the final inning second baseman Al Rubeling was the only Toronto hero with a three-run homer in the third and a run-scoring hit in the seventh. But with one out and nobody on base, Colman and Rubeling got hits and moved around.

Later Grimes, making his debut as a Leaf manager, called on a pinch-hitter who hobbled to the plate on a bad leg and surprised the Giants with a bunt that drove in two runs. Then two successive Toronto batters with 2-0 counts on them switched to the other side of the plate to cope with relief pitchers who had been sent in to take advantage of their original stances.

Wyrostek finished the rally with a single which drove in Ed Mack and Whitey Brandt with two runs for a 10-9 win.

Leafs employed nine managers in the 1940s. Bill Norman and Eddie Sawyer later managed in the majors.

In the 1940s Toronto had a young player named Billy Southworth, whose dad was manager of the world champion St. Louis Cardinals. Southworth was the first professional ball player to enlist, joining the air force. He flew 25 bombing missions over Europe and earned the Distinguished Flying Cross and Air Medal with three Oak Leaf clusters.

He was a lieutenant-colonel in 1945 when he was killed.

The Second World War
ended and crowds returned
to the stadium.

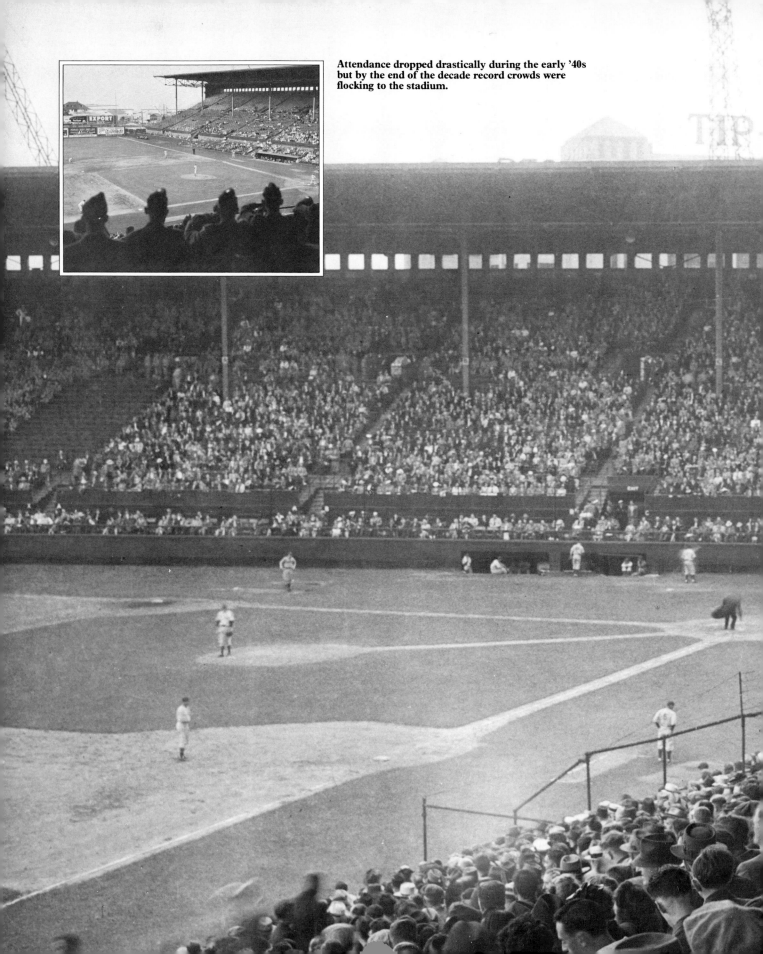

Attendance dropped drastically during the early '40s but by the end of the decade record crowds were flocking to the stadium.

1950-1959

Cooke: The greatest show in the minors

"Three Little Words" was the title of a popular song years ago.

The tune aptly summarizes baseball in Toronto in the Fabulous '50s: JACK KENT COOKE.

The Cooke era in Toronto's baseball history was as flamboyant, exciting and entertaining as the man himself. Cooke made Toronto the greatest city in the minor leagues. To do it, he ran what sometimes looked like a three ring circus.

Sunday baseball was introduced in 1950. Fans flocked to the park. Every night seemed like New Year's Eve. There were fireworks displays and fan appreciation days. Music blared whenever there was a lull on the field and fans left the park with ponies, baseballs, bats, caps and long chunks of salami.

Entertainers visited the park and one comedian dropped to the diamond from a helicopter.

Cooke did everything imaginable to attract fans. He had fantastic success. On two occasions he outdrew a couple of major league teams. More than 3,300,000 people watched baseball in Toronto in the 1950s. Cooke was honored by Sporting News as the minor league executive of the year in 1952 when Leafs attracted 446,040 fans.

Cooke, a Hamilton boy who grew up in the Beaches and attended Malvern Collegiate Institute, was a born salesman, a huckster. He sold encyclopedias from door to door, as well as soap, managed a radio station in Stratford for the late Roy Thomson (he wasn't Lord Thomson of Fleet in those days), and parlayed his magnetic personality into ownership of his own radio station (CKEY) and a string of magazines.

At the ball park he was in total command – almost. From his box seat he had phones connected to the press box and dugout. If something bothered him he'd be on the phone and more than once got into trouble with league offices because of his announcements over the p.a. system.

It was all part of making the ball park the place where things were happening. Fans poured over the Bathurst Street bridge to get there nightly. Ball players won cars for this and that. So did a lucky fan or two. Bathing beauties and models put on fashion shows. Players competed in cow milking contests.

And opening days had all the pomp, pageantry and pizzazz Cooke could muster.

Leafs often were greeted on the steps of the old City Hall on opening day. Often a leggy actress (once Jane Powell), or a personality (skating champion Barbara Ann Scott) tossed out or swung at the first pitch of the season.

Opening day umpires? John Diefenbaker, Fred Gardiner, Allan Lamport, Bill Allen, Nathan Phillips. Politicians and fans flocked to Maple Leaf Stadium because it was THE place to be. In show business vernacular it was a "tough ticket", especially in 1953.

A record 22,216 jammed their way into the park for one game to see big Ed Stevens hit a booming triple to win a 10-inning thriller on opening day.

The Fabulous '50s brought Jack Kent Cooke, pennants and fading major leaguers to Toronto. At Bartow, Fla., for spring training are Cliff Mapes, Cooke, manager Burleigh Grimes, general manager Frank Pollock and Bill Voiselle. The year 1953 wasn't a vintage one as Leafs finished fifth.

To complement the gaudy atmosphere, the ball clubs were winners, too. On July 4, 1951, when Cooke put up $200,000 to purchase 84 percent of the team from Donald Ross and associates, he vowed to give fans an entertaining but winning team, one that would merit their loyalty and support.

It took him a couple of years. But by 1954, with former World Series manager Luke Sewell in command, the Leafs were poised to dominate the International League in a manner similar to the teams of Baltimore and Rochester of earlier eras.

They won the pennant, winning 97 games, and in 1955 missed out by a half-game to Montreal. They bounced back to capture championships with Bruno Betzel in 1956 and Fred (Dixie) Walker the following year.

Montreal again edged them out in 1958. The following season was a disaster as Toronto plummeted to the cellar for the first time in 12 years. But for five glittering years Leaf fans had been treated to the finest show in the minors.

Minors!

It wasn't a word the loquacious Cooke liked to include in his vocabulary. He firmly believed Toronto belonged in the majors. From the day he got into baseball it was his blatant aim to either get the city in the big leagues or purchase a major league franchise for himself.

Meanwhile, Cooke was dedicated to putting on the best show possible. He continually played to the egos of fans.

"Under these portals pass the greatest fans in the world," was one sign which adorned the stadium. He would tell the spectators that "the Maple Leafs are your team and this ball park is your park."

He continually made changes and innovations to increase fan support and convenience and spent his money eagerly to bring in the best players available.

At first he brought in retreads, fading major leaguers who might have one or two more wins in their arms or homers in their bats. Cliff Mapes and Marv Rickert were examples. Eventually he went after border-line major leaguers of proved Triple AAA ability. Cooke had no tieups with major league teams, operating independently, owning most of his own players and borrowing a few as well.

He talked the Yankees into giving him Elston Howard for a year of "seasoning" in 1954. To accomplish the deal he bought a couple of pitchers for more than they were worth. But it was a great deal.

Howard was the hero in his first game in the stadium when his homer gave Leafs a 3-2 win. Ropes were used to hold back the crowd. Scalpers (yes, even ticket scalpers) used to enjoy a lively business on Fleet Street in those days.

Howard hit .330 and was the league's most valuable player.

Cooke also bought or borrowed a bundle of players who later made it up to the majors, but his key performers during the 1950s were Rocky Nelson, Mike Goliat, Lew Morton, Stevens, Archie Wilson, Sam Jethroe, Jim King, Hector Rodriguez and pitchers Bob Tiefenauer, Eddie Blake, Jack Crimian, Lynn Lovenguth, Pat Scantlebury, Humberto Robinson and the Johnsons – Don, Ken and Connie.

You had to admire Cooke's tenacity in his attempts to acquire big league ball for Toronto.

He constantly harangued civic politicians, trying to get a ball park which would attract a major league club. Wherever there was a major league club in trouble Cooke was there, trying to buy. He romanced Lou Perini before the Braves shifted from Boston to Milwaukee and went after the Browns and Athletics before they shuffled off to Baltimore and Kansas City. He offered $5.2 million for the Detroit Tigers when the Briggs family was forced to liquidate its estate.

His last great effort to get this city into the majors came in 1959 when he became one of the founding fathers of the Continental League. Headed by Branch Rickey and Bill Shea, who was chairman, the Continental League was going to be a third major league. It folded, stillborn, a year later when the American League announced plans to expand.

But by this time Cooke had become disenchanted with his chances in Toronto. A year earlier, while commenting on the probability of Toronto winning a third successive title, he said, "The eyes of the entire baseball world will be focused on Toronto and could definitely help us when major league expansion becomes a reality.

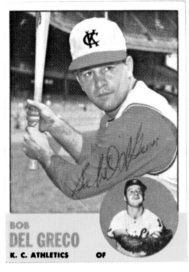

BOB
DEL GRECO
OF
K. C. ATHLETICS

PITCHER
STEVE RIDZIK

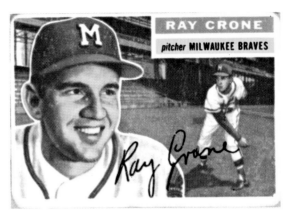

RAY CRONE
pitcher MILWAUKEE BRAVES

FRANK
FUNK
CLEVE. INDIANS P

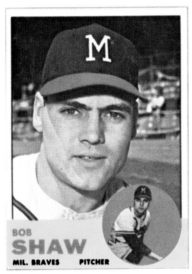

BOB
SHAW
MIL. BRAVES PITCHER

RUDY MINARCIN
pitcher CINCINNATI REDLEGS

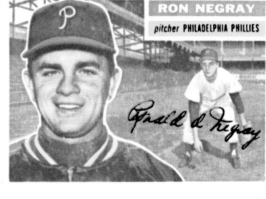

RON NEGRAY
pitcher PHILADELPHIA PHILLIES

JIM
KING
WASH. SENATORS OF

PITCHER
BOB TIEFENAUER

SPORT MAGAZINE
1960
ROOKIE
STAR

KEN JOHNSON KANSAS CITY A'S · PITCHER

Some of the Leafs of the exciting '50s when Toronto outdrew a couple of major league teams. Rocky Nelson was the league's most valuable player in 1958 when he led in hitting, RBIs and home runs; Archie Wilson three times led the team in hitting; the durable Lew Morton, Mike Goliat and Hector Rodriguez; Disappearin' Don Johnson, strikeout artist Ernie Broglio and Stan Jok, who hit three homers in a single game.

Bob Chakales

Lou Kahn

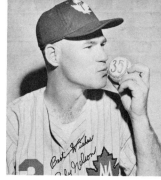

Rocky Nelson

Joe Altobelli

Mike Goliat

Jim King

Hector Rodriguez

Loren Babe

Don Johnson

Lew Morton

Johnny Schmitz

Ernie Broglio

Stan Jok

Ron Negray

Ray Shore

104

Ebba St. Claire

Ed Stevens

Dixie Walker

Archie Wilson

"And, besides, we have the most wonderful fans in the world who deserve the best baseball possible."

But Cooke was dismayed at the entry fee into the majors. He felt it was blackmail. He would have to ante $75,000 apiece for players he felt weren't worth as much or as good as most of his minor league players.

Besides, there was no assurance of a park to play in if he did get himself a franchise. For years Toronto had pussy-footed around the issue as City Hall formed ways and means committees to explore the matter.

Frank (Trader) Lane of the White Sox spelled it out in 1954 at a local welcome the club banquet when he said: "A major league franchise is a civic project. The important thing is to get a stadium, a municipal stadium, and then submit your bid."

The 1950s was an era when Goliat and Morton were identifiable heroes. Each played in over 1,000 games for Leafs. A hard-hitting infielder, Goliat set Leaf career records for most at bats, doubles, home runs and runs batted in while Morton, who learned to hit to every field instead of trying to pull every pitch, scored more runs than any other player in the history of the club.

Nelson, batting from his unprobable stance of pointing both feet at the pitcher, slugged 43 homers in 1958, a team record, hit .326 and drove in 120 runs while winning the MVP award for the second time in his career.

Leafs seemed to have an unending supply of good first basemen in the '50s with Nelson, Stevens, Lou Limmer, Bill Glynn, Les Fleming and Joe Altobelli.

Stevens, the big Texan, three times led the team in RBIs. He thrived on opening day games. In 1952 against Baltimore he hit homers in successive innings, once with the bases loaded in an 8-7 win. Stevens' 10th inning triple before the record crowd in 1953 gave reliefer Ray Shore the win.

It was also Stevens, after doubling, who scored the winning run in Toronto's pennant-winning game in 1956 over Rochester. Rodriguez, the durable shortstop, delivered the game-winning hit.

In 1956 Loren Babe started a triple play with the bases loaded and climaxed the home opener by bouncing a shot off the jeweller's

sign in right field in the 11th inning to give Toronto a 3-2 win over Richmond.

Old Archie, who enjoyed a commendable career with Leafs, was the opening day hero in 1959 when his two-run triple defeated Havana as Crimian got the win over Luis Arroyo.

Wilson was one of three Leafs to hit three homers in a single game in the 1950s. Harry Heslet, who once knocked Leafs out of the playoffs by hitting three-run homers in both ends of a doubleheader in Newark, accomplished the three-homer feat twice in 1950.

In a seven-inning game against Montreal Heslet hit a single and three homers. Three months later in Baltimore the catcher-out-fielder hit a single, double and three homers and knocked in eight runs.

Stan Jok was the other player to hit three out of the park and he did it against Columbus.

Catcher Andy Anderson made the record books in 1951 when he hit two homers in an extra-inning game which Leafs lost. In the 10th he connected for a two-run shot and followed with a solo homer in the 15th. On each occasion Syracuse came back to score two runs.

Toronto had outstanding pitching in the 1950s. Lovenguth, who won 24 games in 1956, became Leafs' first 20-game winner since 1943 when Ol' Luke Hamlin won 21. Lovenguth also had a no-hitter at the stadium that year as he went nine innings against Richmond and allowed three walks. Eleven days earlier Disappearin' Don Johnson tossed a seven-inning no-hitter in Columbus, walking one man.

Johnson won more than 60 games with Toronto over several seasons and might have won more except that he was inclined to take unscheduled vacations from the club.

Three years in a row Toronto pitchers – Crimian, Lovenguth and Johnson – were named the most valuable pitcher in the IL. Eddie Blake was also extremely steady during this period and in one season drove in 17 runs, including all five in a 5-1 win over Buffalo. He hit a homer with the bases full in that contest.

Blake's 66 career wins were the highest for any Leaf pitcher in the 1950s or '60s.

Also outstanding in the '50s were John Hetki, Humberto Robinson, Bob Chakales,

Above: International League champion Leafs of 1957. Top row (left to right): Mike Goliat, Archie Wilson, Cal Abrams, Ebba St. Claire, Loren Babe, Jack Crimian, Sam Jethroe, Don Johnson, Johnny Schmitz. Middle row: Trainer Bill Smith, assistant trainer John Syvulick, Stan Jok, Humberto Robinson, Jim Pearce, Bob Tiefenauer, Ross Grimsley, Rocky Nelson and Charlie Menkes, bat boy. Bottom row: Niles Jordan, Bob Roselli, Lew Morton, coach Lou Kahn, manager Dixie Walker, Hector Rodriguez, Eddie Blake and Jack Daniels.

Top left: Jack Kent Cooke's first Toronto club–1951. Top row (left to right): Irv Medlinger, Les Fleming, Harry Heslet, Charlie White, Leon Day, John Sullivan, John Ostrowski, Charles Grant, Frank Colman, John Crocco, Lew Morton. Middle row: Hal Hudson, Ferrell Anderson, Ray Shore, Elmer Singleton, Russ Bauers, John Hetki, Cliff Fannin, Frank Barnes, coach Fred Collins, Bobby Rhawn, general manager Joe Ziegler. Front row: Bat boy (Unidentified), concessions manager Frank Pollock, broadcaster Joe Crysdale, president Cooke, manager Joe Becker, business manager Bill Houston, promotion manager Max King, Vince Plumbo, Grover Bowers and trainer Bill Smith. In front is batboy Ronnie Stead.

Bottom left: The 1952 Leafs: Top row (left to right): Cec Finkler, Hal Hudson, Harold Keller, Marv Rickert, Ray Shore, Phil Haugstead, Billy DeMars, Ron Stead. Middle row: Business manager Bill Houston, Mike Goliat, John Hetki, Bill Jennings, Red Fahr, Duke Markell, Grower Bowers, coach Frank Colman, Wilmer Fields, trainer Bill Smith. Front row: Vic Lombardi, Ferrell Anderson, Ed Stevens, president Jack Kent Cooke, manager Burleigh Grimes, general manager Frank Pollock, Lew Morton, Stubby Overmire, Bobby Del Greco, Pete Pavlick, Charlie White, secretary-treasurer Neil Watt, promotion manager Max King.

Hal Hudson, Rudy Minarcin, Ernie Broglio, Connie Johnson and Duke Markell. Among clutch relief pitchers, Ray Shore, Pat Scantlebury, Crimian and knuckleballer Bob Tiefenauer were the best.

Tiefenauer was the first relief artist to win both the ERA title (1.89) and top winning percentage (17-5, .733) in the league. Voters, however, overlooked Tief in the balloting for most valuable pitcher as they gave the title to Montreal's Tom Lasorda, who had an 18-6 record and a 2.50 ERA.

Things at the park were rarely dull in the Cooke regime. He often had run-ins with the press. The succession of general managers included Joe Ziegler, Mike Murphy, who resigned four days before the season was to open, Frank Pollock, who had been with the club since 1939 selling programs and concessions, and Rudie Schaffer, now with the White Sox.

Only fellow certain to have a job at the end of the season was Smitty–trainer Bill Smith. He joined the club in 1924 and would be with it until the final game in 1967.

Opening day action at second base. Havana player goes
for double play as he leaps over sliding Toronto runner.

The Stoney's sign (hit the hole and win $2,000 cash) is in background as Milt Smith is about to tag Richmond's Bobby Del Greco.

el Burns

Sam Jethroe (8), one of baseball's fastest men early in his career, slides into third. Coach is Lou Kahn (11).

Above: One of the club's many promotions of the '50s was an Old-Timer's Day. From left: Murph Blandford, Bill Smith, Tim Daly, Frank Colman, Phil Marchildon, Steve O'Neill, Charlie Gehringer, Harry Davis, Tommy Oliver, Ed Sanicki, Red Wingo and Luke Hamlin.

Far left: Sometimes players had to vie with models for attention. From left, Russ Rac, Stan Jok, Bill Antonelli and Mike Goliat don't seem to mind balancing Theresia Hackenberger, Elona Cross, Miss Toronto '57 Marianne Lenchak and Miss Toronto '56 Judy Welch.

Centre: Jack Crimian and his young son Michael. Crimian was league's most valuable pitcher in 1955 with 19 victories.

Left: Guess who's coming for dinner. In 1958 the Leafs and Sam (Shopsy) Shopsowitz (right) treated fans on the diamond. Seated with fans (left) is Rudy Minarcin.

A City Hall reception preceded opening day in the 1950s. From left: Broadcaster Joe Crysdale, general manager Frank Pollock, manager Burleigh Grimes with a 1953 version of a Submarine sandwich, mayor Allan Lamport and owner Jack Kent Cooke.

Rudie Schaffer, with familiar cigar and glasses, was appointed general manager in 1955, replacing Frank Pollock, left. Jack Kent Cooke, right, named Pollock vice-president.

A tall, youthful Elston Howard accepts most popular player trophy in 1954 from Alderman Ken Ostrander. Howard was also MVP in league.

Nothing like a ruckus to enliven a game. Richmond manager Eddie Lopat gets between Leafs' Milt Smith and his players.

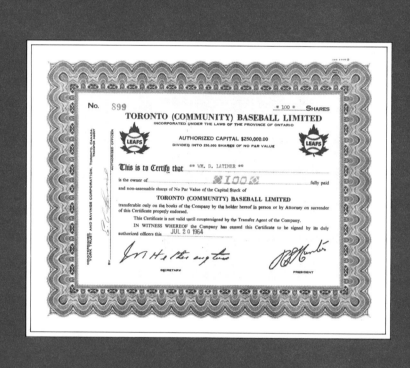

1960-1967

Bottom of the ninth; three out. Game over.

A worthless $100 stock certificate is symbolic of the 1960s. Fans invested in baseball in a futile attempt to save the club. Toronto no longer wanted the minor leagues.

The end was in sight but few baseball people in Toronto had the courage to acknowledge this fact in 1960.

The city had one of its great teams, certainly the best since the remarkable club of 1926 which had opened the stadium then called best in the minor leagues, but now showing its age.

It was creaking and crumbling. Baseball fans no longer flocked there, despite a team that won 100 games and finished 17 games ahead of its closest pursuer, mainly through great pitching and fielding. A run or two was usually enough for the Leafs to win.

No club in the history of the International League ever compiled more than 29 shutouts, not even when schedules were 168 games. But in 154 games in 1960 the Leafs chalked up 32 shutouts in romping to their 12th (and, as it turned out, final) pennant.

However, like the stadium, minor league ball in Toronto was passé. In seven years it finally succumbed because of lack of fan support. In the 1960s two Leaf teams managed by Dick Williams won back-to-back Governor's Cup championships. Attendance dropped each season.

But the fault was not completely with the fans. Fans like to be able to identify with a player; discover his idiosyncrasies; his habits; how he stands at the plate or slides into a base. The characters were disappearing. There was no Ol' Luke (Hot Potato) Hamlin on the mound with his red handkerchief dangling out of his pocket. No Rocky Nelson, pointing his feet towards the mound, spitting tobacco, and then knocking the ball sharply for line drives or homers–hitting feats that made him a star of the 1960 World Series winning Pittsburgh Pirates as well.

In the 1960s players seemed anonymous. Here today and gone tomorrow. They rarely lingered for more than a year or two. The best ones sometimes were gone before the season was over.

In 1963, for instance, 57 players were on Leafs' 20-man roster–almost three full teams. Among the transients were catchers Phil Roof and Rico Carty.

This was the price minor league teams had to pay when they affiliated with major league teams. The big league clubs paid part of the salaries of their chattels and kept them under close surveillance. Toronto paid the first $800 per month of each salary but it had become unprofitable to own players outright. At one time it was a successful way to run a business–developing a player and selling him at a profit.

Jack Kent Cooke did it successfully for seven or eight years after buying the Leafs in 1951 but with rising costs he eventually had to affiliate with a major league team, too.

To conclude that baseball in Toronto was dying you only had to check one set of statistics: Attendance figures for the years 1959 and 1960. In 1959 an eighth place team attracted almost 4,000 more spectators than Mel McGaha's pennant winning Governor's Cup championship team of 1960.

117

Although there had been a regular decline in attendance since the peak year of 1952 (446,040), the 1960 attendance of 203,700 was the smallest since Elmer Yoter's terrible 1947 team which finished eighth.

Baseball, however, did not die gracefully at Maple Leaf Stadium. There was a struggle.

In 1961 Cooke abandoned Toronto for Pebble Beach, Calif., to begin his west coast sports dynasty which eventually included the Los Angeles Kings of the National Hockey League and the Los Angeles Lakers of the National Basketball Association. He also became part owner of the Washington Redskins of the National Football League.

He had given Toronto some exciting years of baseball. For a couple of seasons the club ran on its earlier momentum.

Cooke named Harry Kimber, former Harbor Commission chairman and ex-Toronto Globe and Mail publisher, as president. Cooke became absentee chairman of the board.

The club continued to promote innovatively. But without Cooke most of the promotions were busts. Peter Carnegie, the club's public relations director and statistician for part of the 1960s, recalls two incidents vividly.

"One promotion involved giving away a car. We did everything conceivable to publicize the event. We had a couple of them driving around the city covered with banners and advertised like mad. The papers gave us great coverage. The big day was a holiday doubleheader in summer.

"Beautiful weather. About 3,200 showed up.

"Another time we planned a camera day. We were going to give away a dozen cameras. We told the sponsor about all the advertising and promotion he'd receive. But we got the stall. Finally he told us that 'frankly, we don't care to be associated with the ball club'. That's when I knew it was all over."

By 1964 Cooke wanted out. The losses were growing each year. A group headed by Robert Lawson Hunter and Sam Starr was eager to take over and convert the club into a community-owned team. Later they proposed the sale of a stock issue to the public at $1 a share to save baseball in Toronto.

The plan was to offer 208,000 shares with Starr and Hunter buying 42,000. The shares were available in $10 lots. The new owners were encouraged when more than 3,000 fans showed up for an open house at the stadium.

But less than 100,000 shares of the issue were sold. Prior to the sale of the club Cooke and the Hunter-Starr group haggled over an acceptable figure. Cooke said, "I've invested more than $250,000 in the Leafs. I have never taken out a penny in salary or profit."

Maybe not, but in the 1950s Cooke rarely operated in the red. His year-end sale of players enabled him to show a profit. In the end he sold the club for a reported $50,000, saying it was a major sacrifice to him financially "but inevitable with my leaving Toronto. Absentee ownership doesn't help a team's image. To be successful a club must be the extension of the owner's personality."

For $50,000 the Toronto (Community) Baseball Ltd., organization received six players (Sparky Anderson, Russ Heman, John Anderson, Seth Morehead, Cal Browning and Steve Demeter) and some old equipment.

Hunter was president and Starr vice-president. Both men were long-time baseball fans. Hunter, when he left Bloor Collegiate Institute in 1947, had gone to general manager Arthur Leman and applied for the road secretary's job.

Hunter didn't get the job but he did land one on Bay Street with Percy Gardiner, who had bankrolled the team along with Donald Ross in the 1930s and '40s and who had bought the club after the death of Peter Campbell in 1948.

It was natural that Gardiner would be one of the new organization's directors along with Leon Weinstein, Harry Woolley, Sam Shopsowitz, Frank O'Neill, John Hetherington and Kimber.

Running the affairs of the club were business manager Bill Houston, who had been with the club since 1951, and Frank Pollock, another long time employee who had been put back in the general manager's chair in 1961 after Danny Menendez's one year stint.

The new group was optimistic, especially the spokesman, Hunter.

"Baseball has suffered in Toronto in the last couple of years. We feel public ownership of the team through a stock issue will bring with

A bright, warm afternoon at the park and many of the seats are empty.

Eddie Kasko, who managed Toronto in final year, had few hitters or fans.

The 1960 Leafs, a club loaded with pitching (32 shutouts) and fielding, won 100 games and Governor's Cup. Top row (left to right) Steve Demeter, Herb Plews, Jim King, Wynn Hawkins, Russ Heman, Al Cicotte, Rip Coleman, Stan Kucway, assistant trainer. Middle row: Trainer Bill Smith, Bobby Allen, Pat Scantlebury, Don Dillard, Willie Williams, Joe Hannah, Jackie Waters, Tim Thompson. Bottom row: Bob Chakales, Earl Hersh, Ron Negray, coach Archie Wilson, manager Mel McGaha, Chuck Tanner, Steve Ridzik, Riverboat Smith, Billy Moran, Sparky Anderson.

it more enthusiasm to keep Toronto a pro baseball city. We could have raised $200,000 quite easily ourselves but that would make it our club and not the public's club," he said.

Hunter added, "This ball club isn't going to lose money. Jack Kent Cooke lost money the last couple of years but only because he was trying to run it from California."

But Hunter and Starr knew there were hurdles to clear. They had to build attendance up past the 200,000 mark again if the club was going to break even. The park was also badly in need of repairs. About $75,000 to $100,000 was needed just to stop the hunks of plaster and concrete from falling on already-scarce fans.

The new owners also requested tax and rent relief from the Toronto Harbor Commission, which owned the land the park was on, and from the city. They pointed out that other IL cities with community-sponsored teams were taxed minimal amounts and some didn't even have to pay rent or the maintenance of their parks. (In 1966 maintenance cost Toronto owners $72,415.)

The city did waive its 1966 tax bill of

$33,000 on the promise that the club pay its 1965 taxes of $31,427. Alderman Horace Brown said "this is like reviving a corpse. The fans don't want baseball, not even a championship team."

The Hunter-Starr club lost $168,652 in its first year. Gardiner absorbed most of the debt. In four years the club lost more than $400,000. To worsen matters in the first year a fire destroyed most of the club's records, player contracts and trophies. The outfield fence also blew down.

Hunter had his son Bob doing the public address announcements and cooking hotdogs in the press box. His daughter Elizabeth answered the telephone in the office.

"Things got so bad that whenever we played our annual exhibition game against the Red Sox we'd pray for rain. We had a guarantee with them – gate receipts or a straight $5,000 in case of postponement." It was cheaper to cancel than to open the park.

While Leafs were a flop at the gate in the 1960s they had some excellent teams. Only three teams in Toronto's 79-year history won

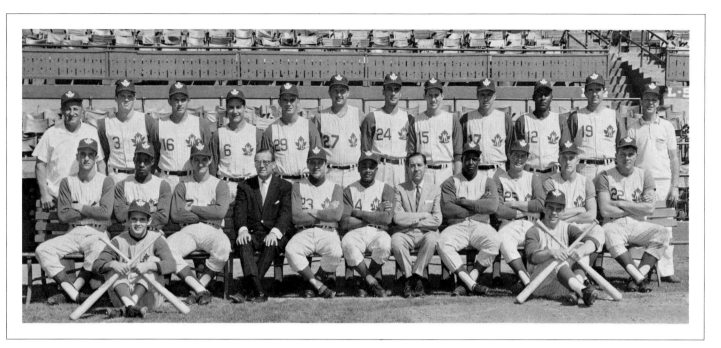

The 1965 Governor's Cup champions: Top row (left to right): Trainer Bill Smith, Mike Andrews, Mickey Sinks, Bob Sadowski, Russ Gibson, Gerry Herron, Gary Waslewski, Bill Rohr, Bill Spanswick, Billy Harrell, Jack Lamabe, assistant trainer Stan Kucway. Front row: Bob Guindon, Stan Johnson, Mike Page, president Bob Hunter, manager Dick Williams, coach Roman Mejias, general manager Bill Houston, Joe Foy, Guido Grilli, Doug Gentry, Mike Ryan. Bat boys Wayne Hamblin and Bill Park.

Toronto's last championship team, Leafs of 1966: Top row (from left): Trainer Bill Smith, Julio Navarro, Mike Page, Jim Russin, Gary Waslewski, Billy Harrell, Billy Rohr and Stan Kucway, assistant trainer. Middle row: Bob Montgomery, Galen Cisco, Stan Johnson, Fred Wenz, Mike Andrews, Gerry Herron, Tony Horton, Pete Magrini, Ed Rakow, Al Lehrer. Bottom row: John Ryan, Owen Johnson, general manager Bill Houston, coach Russ Gibson, president Robert L. Hunter, manager Dick Williams, vice-president Sam Starr, Reggie Smith, Bob Sadowski. Bat boys Mike Carnegie and Don Pyhacz.

100 games, and one was the '60 Leafs. They did it with an amazing pitching staff led by Al Cicotte, Riverboat Smith, Steve Ridzik, Ron Negray and Frank Funk along with Russ Heman, Bob Chakales, Pat Scantlebury and Rip Coleman. Cicotte had eight shutouts, including a masterful 11-inning no-hitter against Montreal. It was a game in which Cicotte almost didn't get out of the first inning. He walked three men but escaped by striking out the side. In the next 10 innings only two men got on base, one by an error.

Lone run of the game followed hits by Jim King, the league's MVP that year with 24 homers, Steve Demeter and Tim Thompson. That year Funk also tossed a no-hitter, a seven-inning gem against Havana.

Cicotte, winning 16 games, had one streak in which he did not allow an earned run in 56 innings. In the playoffs against Buffalo and Rochester he won all three starts, one on a shutout.

Cicotte didn't have it in the Junior World Series against Bill Adair's Louisville Colonels. He was beaten twice. Leafs lost the series in six games. Toronto's two wins came on a four-hitter by Ridzik and a three-hitter by Riverboat. Demeter clouted two homers in each of these wins.

Pittsburgh Pirates' new manager Chuck Tanner, who earlier piloted Chicago White Sox and Oakland A's, was Leafs' leading hitter against the Colonels with a .400 average.

Leafs attempted to lure fans by televising 20 games in 1961 but viewers were more interested in the Major League's Game Of The Week contest. Highlights of that season were Rip Coleman's no-hitter against Richmond, R. C. Stevens' three homers in seven innings against Buffalo and Ellis Burton's amazing feat of hitting two homers in a single inning against Jersey City, one from each side of the plate.

Cooke, who fired Johnny Lipon near the end of the 1961 season, brought in Chuck Dressen in 1962 in an attempt to create interest. Dressen, one of the more successful managers in the majors, was the highest paid

Ex-Leafs met present Leafs in 1963 All-Star game in Buffalo. From left, New York Yankees' Bill Kunkel, Toronto manager Bill Adair, Yankee catcher Elston Howard and Leafs' Jim Coker.

123

manager in the club's history. He did liven things up with the bowls of chili con carne he cooked for his players to eat between games of Sunday doubleheaders. Leafs finished second.

But attendance was still under 200,000. Dressen had a good team which included Neil Chrisley hitting .317, Demeter slugging 26 homers and Jim Constable winning 16 of 20 decisions and posting a 2.56 ERA.

Quiet Bill Adair became manager in '63. The club finished second behind the hitting of Lou Jackson, who batted .315 and 31 homers, and the brilliant fielding of Anderson at second. Jackson and Jim Coker each made the all-star team that year.

Sparky took over in 1964 and there never has been a more sure, confident or honest manager than the umpire-battling second sacker who won numerous fielding titles and five times was voted by managers as the "smartest player in the league."

At his first press conference Sparky announced, "I think I'm going to be a good manager, even outstanding. We won't know until September. If we don't win the pennant then this team will have a new manager next year."

Sparky was a better prophet than manager. He finished fifth. Williams took over in 1965. But Sparky did become a great manager – in the majors with the Cincinnati Reds.

Williams, who went on to win two World Series titles with Oakland, was masterful in Toronto with two ordinary clubs. Both won the Cup. He manipulated his pitching staff magnificently both years and received good seasons from rookies Joe Foy and Reggie Smith. Foy was rookie-of-the-year and led the team in hitting.

Tony Horton and Jim Gosger also were key men at bat along with pitchers Gary Waslewski, Jack Lamabe, Gerry Herron and Ed Rakow.

But it was Russ Gibson, shifted by Williams from behind the plate to first, who powered Toronto to its Cup win over Columbus in 1965. His homer in the opening game was the winning run as Lamabe beat Woody Fryman and Dock Ellis 4-0. Herron shut out the Jets 4-0 in the second game and Gibson knocked in Mike Andrews in Billy Rohr's 1-0 win.

The Toronto managing job eventually landed Sparky Anderson in majors with Cincinnati Reds.

Rip Coleman won a Triumph and 10 games as Leafs' top pitcher in 1961. Handing over keys is Patty Lou Clover.

Handing out bats on Father's Day are Russ Heman and Don Dillard (8) and little Glenn Pollock.

Pitcher Jim Constable was almost as good milking a cow as he was on mound. Led team in wins, percentage and ERA in 1962.

Gibson homered in a 4-3 loss in Columbus but Leafs won the Cup the next night. His two-run homer off Fryman overcame a 3-2 deficit.

Toronto's "final hurrah" came on September 16, 1966, when Horton hit a two-run homer in the 9th inning to beat Richmond 6-5 in the deciding game of the Cup final. Waslewski was the top pitcher in the league, winning 16 games.

Opening days in the 1960s were greeted with 40 degree weather and small crowds. Heroes of these events often were quick to disappear. Pepper Thomas hit a grand-slammer in 1963 and was sold within a month. The following year Harry Chiti clouted a three-run pinch-hit homer to win a 5-3 game and he too was dealt weeks later.

Only 2,211 showed up to see Leafs open their final season. Eddie Kasko was in charge of the Boston Red Sox farm team but he had little in the way of offense as the club finished a distant sixth. John Ryan, a kid from Oshawa, was tops in hitting with .298.

Al Lehrer at short and catcher Jackie Moore led the league on defense and Dave Morehead won 11 games. Dave Vineyard tossed the final no-hitter in the club's history, an untidy affair against Rochester which he won 2-1 despite an error and six walks.

Attendance rarely reached 1,000 that season and on September 4 only 802 fans sauntered through the turnstiles to see Leafs lose 7-2 to Syracuse in the final game at the stadium. Syd O'Brien's two-run homer in the bottom of the ninth was a fitting farewell.

After the game there was talk that Harold Ballard of the hockey Leafs was interested in investing in the club. It was only talk.

Seasonal attendance had drastically declined. Williams' championship 1966 team, which included future major league star Reggie Smith, attracted only 97,000. In 1967 only 67,216 paid for tickets. The club went bankrupt. It was sold to Walter Dilbeck, an Evansville, Ind., real estate developer for $65,000. He took the club and its 79-year history to Louisville, Ky.

With his purchase Dilbeck got three players and a stack of overdue bills for everything from grass fertilizer to hotel bills.

Team president Robert Hunter eyes International League's Governor's Cup which his Leafs won in 1965 and 1966.

— Canada Pictures

— Graphic Artists

When games got quiet the crowd always had super fans Pat Vetere, left, and John (Hoss) Maloney to stir up a little commotion.

— Graphic Artists

Former major league manager Chuck Dressen (left) and playing-coach Tim Thompson in 1962.

And opening day is just four days away. General manager Frank Pollock sweeps off home plate for manager Sparky Anderson

The Hon. John Diefenbaker acts as umpire for catcher Allan Lamport and batter William Allen in 1964.

Resplendent in his chain of office Mayor Nathan Phillips listens to manager Chuck Dressen on steps of Old City Hall in 1962.

Outfielder Jim McKnight had company on western night at park in Bob Hunter, Leon Weinstein, Phil Givens and Sam Shopsowitz, seated.

Opening day was for politicians and fans. Metro chairman Fred Gardiner objects to a high pitch which catcher Joe Hannah reaches for in 1960.

129

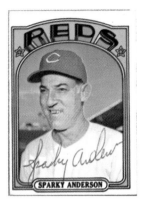

SPARKY ANDERSON

JIM COKER
Catcher
Philadelphia
Phillies

JIM
HANNAN
WASH. SENATORS PITCHER

MACK JONES
Outfield

KUNKE
K.C. Athletics

HOWIE BEDELL
Outfield
Milwaukee
Braves

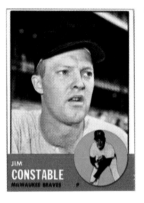

JIM
CONSTABLE
MILWAUKEE BRAVES

BILLY HARRELL
Shortstop
Boston
Red Sox

SAM JONES
Pitcher
San Francisco
Giants

RED SOX
JACK LAMABE
PITCHER

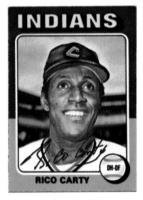

INDIANS

RICO CARTY
DH-OF

CHUCK DRESSEN
Mgr. Milwaukee Braves

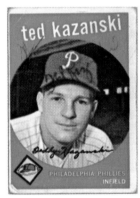

russ heman
CLEVELAND INDIANS
PITCHER

ted kazanski
PHILADELPHIA PHILLIES
INFIELD

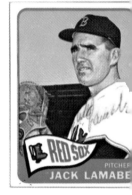

RED SOX
DICK WILLIAMS
of-1b

al cicotte
CLEVELAND INDIANS
PITCHER

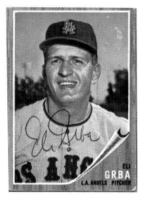

ELI
GRBA
L.A. ANGELS PITCHER

LOU
JOHNSON
MILWAUKEE BRAVES OF

HOWIE
KOPLITZ
DETROIT TIGERS

BRAVES
DENIS MENKE
SS-2nd BASE

billy moran

CLEVELAND INDIANS
SECOND BASE

w. porter

WASHINGTON SENATORS
CATCHER—OUTFIELD

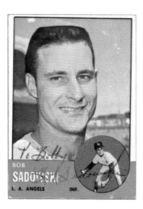

BOB
SADOWSKI

L. A. ANGELS   INF.

RIP COLEMAN

BALTIMORE ORIOLES   PITCHER

SETH MOREHEAD
Pitcher   Chicago Cubs

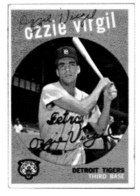

METS

PITCHER
DENNIS RIBANT

ST. LOUIS   OUTFIELD

REGGIE
SMITH   CARDINALS

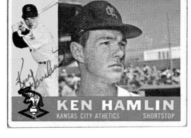

KEN HAMLIN

KANSAS CITY ATHLETICS   SHORTSTOP

BUBBA
MORTON
DETROIT TIGERS   OF

KEN
RETZER
WASH. SENATORS   C

ozzie virgil

DETROIT TIGERS
THIRD BASE

LARRY OSBORNE

DETROIT TIGERS   FIRST BASE

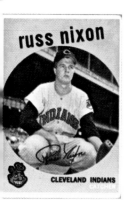

russ nixon

CLEVELAND INDIANS

Twins

PHIL ROOF
CATCHER   TWINS

RED SOX

ROMAN MEJIAS   outfield

CHUCK TANNER

CLEVELAND INDIANS   OUTFIELD

FAYE THRONEBERRY

WASHINGTON SENATORS   OUTFIELD

Fans could
always collect
bubble gum
cards of
ex-Toronto
players.

131

Mel McGaha, one of three Toronto managers to win 100 or more games, was the astute pilot of the 1960 team.

Joe Amalfitano

Al Cicotte

Mike Andrews

Rip Coleman

Steve Demeter

Harry Chiti

Don Dillard

Lou Jackson

Federico (Chi Chi) Olivo

Reggie Smith

Tim Thompson

oe Foy

Ted Kazanski

Orlando Pena

R. C. Stevens

Ozzie Virgil

im Gosger

Sparky Lyle

Pat Scantlebury

Chuck Tanner

Tony Horton

Bob Montgomery

Riverboat Smith

Pepper Thomas

Gary Waslewski

Toronto celebrates in dressing room after crucial win over Richmond which put club into playoffs by half-game over Rochester in 1963. Mayor Don Summerville (left) joins rejoicing along with manager Bill Adair, general manager Frank Pollock and the club's leading hitter, Lou Jackson. Kneeling in front are trainer Bill Smith (left) and Sparky Anderson.

Palm trees flutter in background as Leafs open
1962 training camp at Kelly Field
in Daytona Beach, Fla.

Toronto had 19 pitchers in training camp in 1964 at Daytona Beach.

No team in the history of organized baseball bettered Toronto's pitching staff which recorded 32 shutouts in 1960. From left; Bob (Riverboat) Smith, Rip Coleman, Al Cicotte, Steve Ridzik, Ron Negray and Pat Scantlebury – The Whitewash Crew.

138

Sluggers (from left) Steve Demeter, J. W. Porter, Rocky Nelson, Charley Smith and Lou Jackson.

Outfielders (from left) Charley Smith, J. W. Porter, Corky Withrow, Ellis Burton, Lou Jackson and Don Taussig in Florida.

To make matters worse in the 1960s a fire destroyed most of the club's records, player contracts and trophies.
A despondent general manager, Frank Pollock, surveys damage.

The familiar wrecker's sign went up and down came Maple Leaf Stadium, the short-lived home of Toronto (Community) Baseball.

Seats which had held fans for 41 years occupy the territory once patrolled by Flash Gilhooley, Tommy Oliver, Sam Jethroe and Jackie Waters. The skeletal frame of the once robust stadium is all that remains.

THE HOME OF
TEPERMAN
LEAFS
Toronto Community Baseball

NTRANCE

ENT

NO PARKING
By Order

"There once was a ball park..."

AUTHORIZED BALL
PLAYING ONLY

FOR PERMIT APPLY HARBOURFRONT PROGRAMME
DEPARTMENT 235 QUEENS QUAY WEST

```
         Box Score of Finale
        At Maple Leaf Stadium
  September 4, 1967   Attendance—802
SYRACUSE        AB  R  H  RBI
Shopay, lf       5  1  1   1
Galante, 2b      5  0  1   0
Kennedy, ss      5  1  2   0
Fernandez, c     5  2  3   0
Conde, 1b        4  1  2   1
Tuttle, rf       4  1  2   3
Martz, pr-rf     0  0  0   0
Moschitto, cf    3  1  1   0
Boyer, 3b        3  0  1   0
Bahnsen, p       3  0  0   1
   Totals       37  7 13   6
TORONTO         AB  R  H  RBI
Lehrer, ss       4  1  1   0
O'Brien, 2b      4  1  2   2
Yates, cf        4  0  1   0
Ryan, 3b         4  0  1   0
Calero, 1b       4  0  0   0
Johnson, lf      3  0  1   0
Torchia, rf      3  0  0   0
Montgomery, c    3  0  1   0
Roggenburk, p    2  0  0   0
Rohr, p          0  0  0   0
Russin, ph       1  0  0   0
Wenz, p          0  0  0   0
   Totals       32  2  7   2
SYRACUSE 000 021 130—7 13 0
TORONTO  000 000 002—2  7 2
Errors—Johnson, Lehrer. DP—Syra-
cuse 2, Toronto 2. LOB—Syracuse 6,
Toronto 3. 2b—Boyer, HR—Tuttle
(8th), Shopay (9th), O'Brien (10th).
SF—Bahnsen.
                IP  H  R  ER  SO  BB
Bahnsen
  (W, 9-11)      9  7  2  2   5   0
Roggenburk
  (L, 5-10)      7 10  6  4   2   1
Rohr             1  2  1  1   1   1
Wenz             1  1  0  0   0   0
Roggenburk pitched to 2 batters in
8th inning.
Time: 1:46.
```

Toronto Baseball Statistics
1885-1967

Toronto
Year-by-Year

Year	Manager	Won-Lost	Pct.	Pos.	Attendance
1967	Eddie Kasko (64-72)	65-75	.460	6th	67,216
	Jackie Moore (1-3)				
1966	Dick Williams	82-65	.558	2nd	96,918
1965	Dick Williams	81-64	.559	3rd	118,310
1964	Sparky Anderson	80-72	.526	5th	144,785
1963	Bill Adair	76-75	.503	2nd	119,596
1962	Chuck Dressen	91-62	.595	2nd	193,656
1961	John Lipon (51-56)	76-79	.490	5th	150,960
	Tim Thompson (25-23)				
1960	Mel McGaha	100-54	.649	1st	203,700
1959	Fred (Dixie) Walker (65-81)	69-85	.448	8th	207,505
	Lou Kahn (4-4)				
1958	Fred (Dixie) Walker	87-65	.572	2nd	281,971
1957	Fred (Dixie) Walker	88-65	.575	1st	342,597
1956	Bruno Betzel	86-66	.566	1st	315,161
1955	Luke Sewell	94-59	.614	2nd	350,742
1954	Luke Sewell	97-57	.630	1st	389,707
1953	Burleigh Grimes	78-76	.506	5th	382,432
1952	Joe Becker (44-44)	78-76	.506	4th	446,040
	Burleigh Grimes (34-32)				
1951	Joe Becker	77-76	.503	5th	296,847
1950	Jack Sanford	60-90	.400	7th	226,951
1949	Del Bissonette	80-72	.526	5th	353,247
1948	Ed Sawyer (48-47)	78-76	.506	5th	291,977
	Dick Porter (30-29)				
1947	Elmer Yoter	64-90	.416	8th	171,730
1946	Harry Davis (22-28)	71-82	.464	6th	182,191
	Bill Norman (49-54)				
1945	Harry Davis	85-67	.559	3rd	204,953
1944	Burleigh Grimes	79-74	.516	3rd	165,685
1943	Burleigh Grimes	95-57	.625	1st	185,456
1942	Burleigh Grimes	74-79	.484	6th	178,327
1941	Lena Blackburne	47-107	.305	8th	57,815
1940	Tony Lazzeri	57-101	.361	8th	67,123
1939	Jack Burns (19-38)	63-90	.412	8th	119,074
	Tony Lazzeri (44-52)				
1938	Dan Howley (24-37)	72-81	.471	5th	109,417
	Jack Burns (48-44)				
1937	Dan Howley	63-88	.417	7th	144,157
1936	Isaac (Ike) Boone	77-76	.503	5th	105,897
1935	Isaac (Ike) Boone	78-76	.506	6th	126,928
1934	Isaac (Ike) Boone	85-67	.559	3rd	136,301
1933	Dan Howley	82-85	.491	5th	109,258
1932	Tom Daly (24-43)	54-113	.323	8th	49,963
	Lena Blackburne (30-70)				
1931	Steve O'Neill	83-84	.497	5th	102,143
1930	Steve O'Neill	87-80	.521	4th	121,431
1929	Steve O'Neill	92-76	.548	2nd	163,862
1928	Bill O'Hara	86-80	.518	3rd	202,864
1927	Lee Fohl (42-39)	89-78	.533	4th	124,098
	Bill O'Hara (47-39)				
1926	Dan Howley	109-57	.657	1st	221,846
1925	Dan Howley	99-63	.611	2nd	115,592
1924	Dan Howley	98-67	.594	2nd	102,153
1923	Dan Howley	81-79	.506	4th	114,908
1922	Eddie Onslow	76-88	.463	5th	119,608
1921	Larry Doyle (47-46)	89-77	.536	4th	147,639
	Lena Blackburne (42-31)				
1920	Hugh Duffy	108-46	.701	2nd	207,570
1919	George Gibson	93-57	.620	2nd	
1918	Dan Howley	88-39	.693	1st	
1917	Larry Lajoie	93-61	.604	1st	
1916	Joe Birmingham (55-53)	73-66	.525	5th	
	Lena Blackburne (18-13)				
1915	William J. Clymer	72-67	.518	3rd	
1914	Joseph Kelley	74-70	.514	4th	
1913	Joseph Kelley	70-83	.458	7th	
1912	Joseph Kelley	91-62	.596	1st	
1911	Joseph Kelley	94-59	.614	3rd	
1910	Joseph Kelley	80-72	.526	4th	
1909	Joseph Kelley	75-68	.524	4th	
1908	Mike Kelley (37-39)	59-79	.428	6th	
	Larry Schlafly (22-40)				
1907	Joseph Kelley	83-51	.619	1st	
1906	Edward Barrow	46-88	.343	8th	
1905	Richard Harley (42-65)	48-89	.350	8th	
	Jack White (6-24)				
1904	Arthur Irwin (29-36)	67-71	.486	6th	
	Richard Harley (38-35)				
1903	James A. Gardner	82-45	.646	3rd	
1902	Edward G. Barrow	85-42	.669	1st	
1901	Edward G. Barrow	76-50	.603	2nd	
1900	Edward G. Barrow	64-68	.485	5th	
1899	Wally Taylor	58-57	.504	4th	
1898	Arthur Irwin	64-55	.538	3rd	
1897	Arthur Irwin	75-52	.591	2nd	
1896	Al Buckenberger	59-57	.509	4th	
1895	Charles Maddock (14-34)	43-76	.361	7th	
	Jack Chapman (29-42)				
1890	Charles Maddock	30-20	.600	3rd	
1889	Charles H. Cushman	54-54	.500	5th	
1888	Charles H. Cushman	76-36	.679	2nd	
1887	Charles H. Cushman	65-36	.644	1st	
1886	John H. Humphries	53-41	.563	3rd	
1885	Harrison L. Spence	24-20	.545	3rd	

Governor's Cup Champions

Year		Manager
1966	Toronto 4, Richmond 1 (Final)	Dick Williams
	Toronto 3, Columbus 2 (Semi-final)	
1965	Toronto 4, Columbus 2 (Final)	Dick Williams
	Toronto 4, Atlanta 0 (Semi-final)	
1960	Toronto 4, Rochester 1 (Final)	Mel McGaha
	Toronto 4, Buffalo 0 (Semi-final)	
1934	Toronto 4, Rochester 1 (Final)	Ike Boone
	Toronto 4, Newark 3 (Semi-final)	

Finalists

Year		Manager
1958	Toronto 4, Rochester 1 (Semi-final)	Dixie Walker
	Montreal 4, Toronto 1 (Final)	
1956	Toronto 4, Montreal 1 (Semi-final)	Bruno Betzel
	Rochester 4, Toronto 3 (Final)	
1955	Toronto 4, Havana 1 (Semi-final)	Luke Sewell
	Rochester 4, Toronto 0 (Final)	
1943	Toronto 4, Montreal 0 (Semi-final)	Burleigh Grimes
	Syracuse 4, Toronto 2 (Final)	

Junior World Series Champions

Year		Manager
1907	Toronto 4, Columbus 1	Joseph Kelley
1926	Toronto 5, Louisville 0	Dan Howley

Finalists

Year		Manager
1917	Indianapolis 4, Toronto 1	Larry Lajoie
1934	Columbus 5, Toronto 4	Ike Boone
1960	Louisville 4, Toronto 2	Mel McGaha

Toronto Pennant Winners

Year	Record	Pct.	Manager
1960	100-54	.649	Mel McGaha
1957	88-65	.575	Dixie Walker
1956	86-66	.566	Bruno Betzel
1954	97-57	.630	Luke Sewell
1943	95-57	.625	Burleigh Grimes
1926	109-57	.657	Dan Howley
1918	88-39	.693	Dan Howley
1917	93-61	.604	Larry Lajoie
1912	91-62	.595	Joseph Kelley
1907	83-51	.619	Joseph Kelley
1902	85-42	.669	Edward Barrow
1887	65-36	.644	Charles Cushman

Toronto Players or Managers elected to International League Hall of Fame

	Years with Toronto
John Berly	1936-1940
Bruno Betzel	1954-1956
Ike Boone	1933-1936
Jack Dunn	1896
Luke Hamlin	1933, 1943-1948
Dan Howley	1918, 1923-1926, 1933, 1937-1939
Rocky Nelson	1957-1958, 1962
Steve O'Neill	1926, 1929-1931
Ed Onslow	1918-1924
Dick Porter	1948
Dick Rudolph	1907-1912
George Selkirk	1932
George Stallings	1887
Fred (Dixie) Walker	1931, 1957-1959

International League Honor Roll Toronto Maple Leafs

Most Valuable Player	
1934	Isaac (Ike) Boone
1954	Elston Howard
1956	Mike Goliat
1958	Rocky Nelson
1960	Jim King
1965	Joe Foy

Most Valuable Pitcher	
1955	Jack Crimian
1956	Lynn Lovenguth
1957	Don Johnson
1960	Al Cicotte
1966	Gary Waslewski

Rookie-Of-The-Year	
1965	Joe Foy

Former Leafs in Baseball's Hall of Fame

EDWARD GRANT BARROW
CLUB EXECUTIVE, MANAGER, LEAGUE PRESIDENT IN MINORS AND MAJORS FROM 1894 TO 1945. CONVERTED BABE RUTH FROM PITCHER TO OUTFIELDER AS MANAGER BOSTON A.L. IN 1918. DISCOVERED HONUS WAGNER AND MANY OTHER GREAT STARS. WON WORLD SERIES IN 1918. BUILT NEW YORK YANKEES INTO OUTSTANDING ORGANIZATION IN BASEBALL AS BUSINESS MANAGER FROM 1920 TO 1945, WINNING 14 PENNANTS, 10 WORLD SERIES.

DAN BROUTHERS
HARD-HITTING FIRST BASEMAN OF EIGHT MAJOR LEAGUE CLUBS, HE WAS PART OF ORIGINAL "BIG FOUR" OF BUFFALO. TRADED WITH OTHER MEMBERS OF THAT COMBINATION TO DETROIT, HE HIT .419 AS CITY WON ITS ONLY NATIONAL LEAGUE CHAMPIONSHIP IN 1887.

HUGH DUFFY
BRILLIANT AS A DEFENSIVE OUTFIELDER FOR THE BOSTON NATIONALS, HE COMPILED A BATTING AVERAGE IN 1894 WHICH WAS NOT TO BE CHALLENGED IN HIS LIFETIME • .438.

CHARLES L. GEHRINGER
SECOND BASEMAN WITH DETROIT A.L. FROM 1925 THROUGH 1941 AND COACH IN 1942. COMPILED LIFETIME BATTING AVERAGE OF .321 IN 2323 GAMES, COLLECTED 2839 HITS. NAMED MOST VALUABLE PLAYER IN A.L. IN 1937. BATTED .321 IN WORLD SERIES COMPETITION AND HAD A .500 AVERAGE FOR SIX ALL-STAR GAMES.

BURLEIGH ARLAND GRIMES
1916 — 1934
ONE OF THE GREAT SPITBALL PITCHERS. WON 270 GAMES, LOST 212 FOR 7 MAJOR LEAGUE CLUBS. FIVE 20 VICTORY SEASONS. WON 13 IN ROW FOR GIANTS IN 1927. MANAGED DODGERS IN 1937 AND 1938. LIFETIME E.R.A. 3.52.

CARL HUBBELL
NEW YORK N.L. 1928 - 1943
HAILED FOR IMPRESSIVE PERFORMANCE IN 1934 ALL-STAR GAME WHEN HE STRUCK OUT RUTH, GEHRIG, FOXX, SIMMONS AND CRONIN IN SUCCESSION. NICKNAMED GIANTS' MEAL-TICKET. WON 253 GAMES IN MAJORS, SCORING 16 STRAIGHT IN 1936. COMPILED STREAK OF 46 1/3 SCORELESS INNINGS IN 1933. HOLDER OF MANY RECORDS.

WILLIE KEELER
"HIT 'EM WHERE THEY AIN'T!"
BASEBALL'S GREATEST PLACE-HITTER; BEST BUNTER. BIG LEAGUE CAREER 1892 TO 1910 WITH N.Y. GIANTS, BALTIMORE ORIOLES, BROOKLYN SUPERBAS, N.Y. HIGHLANDERS. NATIONAL LEAGUE BATTING CHAMPION '97-'98.

JOSEPH JAMES KELLEY
1891 - 1908
STANDOUT HITTER AND LEFT FIELDER OF CHAMPION 1894-95-96 BALTIMORE ORIOLES AND 1899-1900 BROOKLYN SUPERBAS. BATTED OVER .300 FOR 11 CONSECUTIVE YEARS WITH HIGH OF .391 IN 1894. EQUALLED RECORD WITH 9 HITS IN 9 AT-BATS IN DOUBLEHEADER. ALSO PLAYED FOR BOSTON, PITTSBURGH AND CINCINNATI OF N.L. AND BALTIMORE OF A.L. MANAGED CINCINNATI 1902 TO 1905 AND BOSTON N.L. IN 1908.

RALPH McPHERRAN KINER
PITTSBURGH, N.L. CHICAGO, N.L. CLEVELAND, A.L. 1946 - 1955
HIT 369 HOME RUNS AND AVERAGED BETTER THAN 100 RUNS BATTED IN PER SEASON IN TEN-YEAR CAREER. ONLY PLAYER TO LEAD HIS LEAGUE OR SHARE LEAD IN HOMERS SEVEN YEARS IN A ROW, 1946-1952. TWICE HAD MORE THAN 50 IN SEASON. SET N.L. MARK OF 101 FOUR-BAGGERS IN TWO SUCCESSIVE YEARS WITH 54 IN 1949 AND 47 IN 1950. LED N.L. IN SLUGGING PCT. THREE TIMES.

NAPOLEON (LARRY) LAJOIE
PHILADELPHIA (N) 1896-1900
PHILADELPHIA (A) 1901
CLEVELAND (A) 1902-14
PHILADELPHIA (A) 1915 - 16
GREAT HITTER AND MOST GRACEFUL AND EFFECTIVE SECOND-BASEMAN OF HIS ERA. MANAGED CLEVELAND 4 YEARS. LEAGUE BATTING CHAMPION 1901-03-04.

HENRY EMMET MANUSH
1923 — 1939
SLUGGING OUTFIELDER FOR 6 MAJOR LEAGUE CLUBS. BATTING CHAMPION OF A.L. AT .378 WITH 1926 TIGERS. LIFETIME AVERAGE OF .330 IN 2,009 MAJOR LEAGUE GAMES. HAD 2,524 HITS.

Toronto Players, Managers and Canadians who managed in the Major Leagues

George (Sparky) Anderson	Cincinnati (NL)	1970–
Edward G. Barrow	Detroit (AL)	1903-1904
	Boston (AL)	1918-1920
Joe Birmingham	Cleveland (AL)	1912-1915
Del Bissonette	Boston (NL)	1945
R. (Lena) Blackburne	Chicago (AL)	1928-1929
William Bradley	Brooklyn (FL)	1914
Albert Buckenberger	Columbus (AA)	1889-1890
	Pittsburgh (NL)	1892-1894
	St. Louis (NL)	1895
	Boston (NL)	1902-1904
Bill Carrigan	Boston (AL)	1913-1916
	Boston (AL)	1927-1929
John C. Chapman	Louisville (NL)	1877
	Milwaukee (NL)	1878
	Worcester (NL)	1882
	Detroit (NL)	1883-1884
	Buffalo (NL)	1885
	Louisville (AA)	1889-1891
	Louisville (NL)	1892
Charles Cushman	Milwaukee (AA)	1891
Chuck Dressen	Cincinnati (NL)	1934-1937
	Brooklyn (NL)	1951-1953
	Washington (AL)	1955-1957
	Milwaukee (NL)	1960-1961
	Detroit (AL)	1963-1966
Hugh Duffy	Milwaukee (AL)	1901
	Philadelphia (NL)	1904-1906
	Chicago (AL)	1910-1911
	Boston (AL)	1921-1922
Bob Elliott	Kansas City (AL)	1960
Jay Faatz	Cleveland (PL)	1890
Lee Fohl	Cleveland (AL)	1915-1919
	St. Louis (AL)	1921-1923
	Boston (AL)	1924-1926
George (Moon) Gibson	Pittsburgh (NL)	1920-1922
	Chicago (NL)	1925
	Pittsburgh (NL)	1932-1934
Burleigh Grimes	Brooklyn (NL)	1937-1938
Dan Howley	St. Louis (AL)	1927-1929
	Cincinnati (NL)	1930-1932
Arthur Irwin	Washington (NL)	1889
	Boston (AA)	1891
	Washington (NL)	1892
	Philadelphia (NL)	1894-1895
	New York (NL)	1896
	Washington (NL)	1898-1899
Ed Kasko	Boston (AL)	1970-1973
Joe Kelley	Cincinnati (NL)	1902-1905
	Boston (NL)	1908
Napoleon (Larry) Lajoie	Cleveland (AL)	1905-1909
Fred Lake	Boston (AL)	1908-1909
	Boston (NL)	1910
Johnny Lipon	Cleveland (AL)	1971
Mel McGaha	Cleveland (AL)	1962
	Kansas (AL)	1964-1965
J. T. (Deacon) McGuire	Washington (NL)	1898
	Boston (AL)	1907-1908
	Cleveland (AL)	1909-1911
Fred Mitchell	Chicago (NL)	1917-1920
	Boston (NL)	1921-1923
Bill Norman	Detroit (AL)	1958-1959
Steve O'Neill	Cleveland (AL)	1935-1937
	Detroit (AL)	1943-1948
	Boston (AL)	1950-1951
	Philadelphia (NL)	1952-1954
Eddie Sawyer	Philadelphia (NL)	1948-1952
	Philadelphia (NL)	1958-1960
Larry Schlafly	Buffalo (FL)	1914-1915
Luke Sewell	St. Louis (AL)	1941-1946
	Cincinnati (NL)	1950-1951
Jack Slattery	Boston (NL)	1928
Mayo Smith	Philadelphia (NL)	1955-1958
	Detroit (AL)	1967-1970
Harrison L. Spence	Indianapolis (NL)	1888
George Stallings	Philadelphia (NL)	1897-1898
	Detroit (AL)	1901
	New York (AL)	1909-1910
	Boston (NL)	1913-1920
Chuck Tanner	Chicago (AL)	1971-1975
	Oakland (AL)	1976
	Pittsburgh (NL)	1977–
William H. Watkins	Indianapolis (AA)	1884
	Detroit (NL)	1885-1888
	Kansas City (AA)	1888-1889
	St. Louis (NL)	1893
	New York (NL)	1895
	Pittsburgh (NL)	1888-89
Dick Williams	Boston (AL)	1967-1969
	Oakland (AL)	1971-1973
	California (AL)	1974-1975
	Montreal (NL)	1977–

Toronto Managers

200 wins or more

Dan Howley	644
Joseph Kelley	567
Burleigh Grimes	360
Edward G. Barrow	271
Steve O'Neill	262
Dixie Walker	240
Ike Boone	240
Arthur Irwin	206

The .700 Club

Hugh Duffy	.701

The .600 Club

Mel McGaha	.649
James A. Gardner	.646
Luke Sewell	.622
George Gibson	.620
Charles Cushman	.607
Napoleon (Larry) Lajoie	.604

Former Toronto Players
or Managers
who managed
World Series Teams

1914	Boston	(NL)	GEORGE STALLINGS	4-0	Philadelphia	(AL)	Connie Mack
1915	Boston	(AL)	BILL CARRIGAN	4-1	Philadelphia	(NL)	Pat Moran
1916	Boston	(AL)	BILL CARRIGAN	4-1	Brooklyn	(NL)	Wilbert Robinson
1918	Boston	(AL)	ED BARROW	4-2	Chicago	(NL)	FRED MITCHELL
1944	St. Louis	(NL)	Billy Southworth	4-2	St. Louis	(AL)	LUKE SEWELL
1945	Detroit	(AL)	STEVE O'NEILL	4-3	Chicago	(NL)	Charlie Grimm
1950	New York	(AL)	Casey Stengel	4-0	Philadelphia	(NL)	ED SAWYER
1952	New York	(AL)	Casey Stengel	4-3	Brooklyn	(NL)	CHUCK DRESSEN
1953	New York	(AL)	Casey Stengel	4-2	Brooklyn	(NL)	CHUCK DRESSEN
1967	St. Louis	(NL)	Red Schoendienst	4-3	Boston	(AL)	DICK WILLIAMS
1970	Baltimore	(AL)	Earl Weaver	4-1	Cincinnati	(NL)	SPARKY ANDERSON
1972	Oakland	(AL)	DICK WILLIAMS	4-3	Cincinnati	(NL)	SPARKY ANDERSON
1973	Oakland	(AL)	DICK WILLIAMS	4-3	New York	(NL)	Yogi Berra
1975	Cincinnati	(NL)	SPARKY ANDERSON	4-3	Boston	(AL)	Darrell Johnson
1976	Cincinnati	(NL)	SPARKY ANDERSON	4-0	New York	(AL)	Billy Martin

Toronto players or managers capitalized

Toronto Managers
(1885-1967)

	Years	Won	Lost	Pct.
William Adair	1963	76	75	.503
Sparky Anderson	1964	80	72	.526
Edward Barrow	1900-02, 1906	271	248	.522
Joseph Becker	1951-52	121	120	.502
Bruno Betzel	1956	86	66	.566
Joseph Birmingham	1916	55	53	.509
Del Bissonette	1949	80	72	.526
Lena Blackburne	1916, 1921, 1932, 1941	137	221	.383
Ike Boone	1934-36	240	219	.523
Al Buckenberger	1896	59	57	.509
Jack Burns	1938-39	67	82	.450
John Chapman	1895	29	42	.408
William Clymer	1915	72	67	.518
Charles Cushman	1887-1889	195	126	.607
Tom Daly	1932	24	43	.358
Harry Davis	1945-46	107	95	.530
Larry Doyle	1921	47	46	.505
Chuck Dressen	1962	91	62	.595
Hugh Duffy	1920	108	46	.701
Lee Fohl	1927	42	39	.519
James Gardner	1903	82	45	.646
George Gibson	1919	93	57	.620
Burleigh Grimes	1942-44, 1952-53	360	318	.531
Richard Harley	1904-05	80	100	.444
Dan Howley	1918, 1923-26, 1933, 1937-38	644	515	.556
John Humphries	1886	53	41	.563
Arthur Irwin	1897-98, 1904	206	178	.536
Lou Kahn	1959	4	4	.500
Eddie Kasko	1967	64	72	.471
Joseph Kelley	1907, 1909-14	567	465	.549
Michael Kelley	1908	37	39	.487
Nap Lajoie	1917	93	61	.604
Tony Lazzeri	1939-40	101	153	.398
Johnny Lipon	1961	51	56	.477
Charles Maddock	1890, 1895	44	54	.449
Mel McGaha	1960	100	54	.649
Jackie Moore	1967	1	3	.250
Bill Norman	1946	49	54	.476
William O'Hara	1927-28	133	119	.528
Steve O'Neill	1929-31	262	240	.522
Eddie Onslow	1922	76	88	.463
Richard Porter	1948	30	29	.508
Jack Sanford	1950	60	90	.400
Eddie Sawyer	1948	48	47	.505
Larry Schlafly	1908	22	40	.355
Luke Sewell	1954-55	191	116	.622
Harrison Spence	1885	24	20	.545
Wally Taylor	1899	58	57	.504
Tim Thompson	1961	25	23	.521
Dixie Walker	1957-59	240	211	.532
Jack White	1905	6	24	.200
Dick Williams	1965-66	163	129	.558
Elmer Yoter	1947	64	90	.416

Toronto's No-Hit Heroes

William Stemmeyer

June 25, 1885		R	H	E
Toronto	401 000 100	6	6	4
Hamilton	102 100 000	4	0	18

Stemmeyer and Miller; (Hamilton Clippers battery not available).

Fred Mitchell

July 6, 1908				
Toronto	000 000 011	2	3	1
Montreal	000 000 000	0	0	3

Mitchell and Pierce; Stanley and Ball.

Dick Rudolph

September 12, 1910 (No-hitter for 10 innings).

Montreal	000 000 000 000	0	2	0
Toronto	000 000 000 001	1	6	2

Winter and Hardy; Rudolph and Tonneman.

Urban Shocker

July 22, 1916				
Toronto	000 000 000 01	1	7	3
Rochester	000 000 000 00	0	0	1

Shocker and Kelly; Leverenz and Clarke, Hale.

Claude Satterfield

July 29, 1924				
Jersey City	000 000 0	0	0	0
Toronto	000 010 x	1	4	1

Barnhardt and Kennick; Satterfield and Sullivan.

John Prudhomme

August 23, 1927				
Reading	000 000 000	0	0	1
Toronto	330 130 04x	14	14	0

Watson, Hansen and Hill; Prudhomme and Styles.

John Prudhomme

August 22, 1928				
Jersey City	000 000 0	0	0	1
Toronto	010 004 x	5	5	1

Henderson, Higgins and Head; Prudhomme and Styles.

Leroy Herrmann

May 2, 1936				
Newark	000 000 000 0	0	0	1
Toronto	000 000 000 1	1	7	2

Duke and Baker; Herrmann and Erickson.

William Weir

May 16, 1939				
Baltimore	000 000 000	0	0	1
Toronto	100 030 31x	8	10	2

Davis, Hudson and West; Weir and Harshany.

Tom Ananicz

September 6, 1943				
Buffalo	000 000 0	0	0	1
Toronto	000 000 1	1	7	0

Parkhurst and Denning; Ananicz and Crompton.

Oscar Judd

June 14, 1948				
Toronto	000 006 1	7	9	1
Syracuse	000 000 0	0	0	0

Judd and Plumbo; Howell, Erickson, Bebber and Bosiack.

Al Porto

May 7, 1949				
Newark	000 000 0	0	0	1
Toronto	300 110 x	5	4	1

Tefft, Gorman, Mitchell and Heslet. Porto and Heyman.

Don Johnson

June 5, 1956				
Toronto	000 020 0	2	7	0
Columbus	000 000 0	0	0	0

Johnson and Sawatski; Ceccarelli, Miller (7) and Shantz.

Lynn Lovenguth

June 16, 1956				
Richmond	000 000 000	0	0	0
Toronto	002 042 00x	8	11	0

Post, Kraly and Watlington; Lovenguth and Sawatski.

Frank Funk

June 16, 1960				
Havana	000 000 0	0	0	0
Toronto	001 000 x	1	3	0

Miller and Izquierdo; Funk and Jones.

Al Cicotte

September 3, 1960				
Montreal	000 000 000 00	0	0	1
Toronto	000 000 000 01	1	10	1

Kunkel and Coleman; Cicotte and Thompson.

Rip Coleman

July 1, 1961				
Richmond	000 000 0	0	0	3
Toronto	001 002 x	3	3	0

Carpin and Gonder; Coleman and Hannah.

Dave Vineyard

May 23, 1967				
Rochester	000 001 000	1	0	0
Toronto	000 101 000	2	5	1

Fisher, Delgado (7) and Carreon; Vineyard and Moore.

Toronto's Leading Pitchers

Year	Wins		Percentage			Earned Run Average	
1967	Dave Morehead	11	Dave Morehead	11-5	.688	Gary Waslewski	2.16
1966	Gary Waslewski	18	Ed Rakow	11-4	.733	Gary Waslewski	2.52
1965	Gerry Herron	11	Jack Lamabe	10-3	.769	Jack Lamabe	1.95
1964	Ron Piche	14	Ron Piche	14-3	.824	Jim Bronstad	2.74
1963	Carl Bouldin	10	Carl Bouldin	10-8	.556	Carl Bouldin	3.42
1962	Jim Constable	16	Jim Constable	16-4	.800	Jim Constable	2.56
1961	Steve Ridzik	11	Rip Coleman	10-7	.588	Rip Coleman	2.42
1960	AL CICOTTE	16	Riverboat Smith	14-6	.700	AL CICOTTE	1.79
1959	Bob Chakales	13	Pat Scantlebury	12-5	.706	Pat Scantlebury	3.07
1958	Bob Tiefenauer	17	BOB TIEFENAUER	17-5	.773	BOB TIEFENAUER	1.89
1957	HUMBERTO ROBINSON	18	Humberto Robinson	18-7	.720	Humberto Robinson	2.95
1956	LYNN LOVENGUTH	24	Lynn Lovenguth	24-12	.667	Lynn Lovenguth	2.68
1955	Jack Crimian	19	Connie Johnson	12-2	.857	Jack Crimian	2.10
1954	Connie Johnson	17	Rudy Minarcin	11-2	.846	Connie Johnson	3.72
1953	Don Johnson	15	Vic Lombardi	11-8	.579	Don Johnson	2.67
1952	Duke Markell	14	John Hetki	13-7	.650	John Hetki	2.91
1951	JOHN HETKI	19	Hal Hudson	16-5	.762	John Hetki	2.85
1950	Jocko Thompson	10	Jocko Thompson	10-14	.417	Paul Stuffel	3.99
1949	Bubba Church	15	Jocko Thompson	14-5	.737	Bubba Church	2.35
1948	Oscar Judd	14	Oscar Judd	14-8	.636	Oscar Judd	4.79
1947	Luke Hamlin	15	Luke Hamlin	15-6	.714	Luke Hamlin	2.22
1946	Joe Coleman	14	Bill McCahan	11-7	.611	Bill McCahan	2.76
1945	Luke Hamlin	16	Woody Crowson	13-8	.619	Luke Hamlin	3.22
1944	Al Jarlett	18	Al Jarlett	18-9	.667	WOODY CROWSON	2.41
1943	Luke Hamlin	21	Luke Hamlin	21-8	.724	Luke Hamlin	1.96
1942	Bill Brandt	15	Bill Brandt	15-11	.577	Nick Strincevich	2.40
1941	Porter Vaughan	12	Porter Vaughan	12-12	.500	Dick Fowler	3.30
			Dick Fowler	10-10	.500		
1940	Carl Fischer	10	Carl Fischer	10-12	.455	Carl Fischer	2.53
	Phil Marchildon	10					
1939	Carl Fischer	11	Carl Fischer	11-9	.550	John Berly	2.21
	John Pezzullo	11					
1938	JOE SULLIVAN	18	Joe Sullivan	18-10	.643	Joe Mulligan	3.21
1937	Woody Davis	13	Woody Davis	13-13	.500	Joe Mulligan	3.26
1936	Leroy Herrmann	16	Jake Mooty	12-8	.600	Silas Johnson	2.38
1935	Walter Hilcher	19	Jim Pattison	16-8	.667	Jim Pattison	3.73
1934	Gene Schott	18	Gene Schott	18-9	.667	Gene Schott	3.76
1933	Luke Hamlin	21	Ralph Birkofer	16-8	.667	Luke Hamlin	3.48
1932	Guy Cantrell	14	Arthur Smith	11-13	.458	Arthur Smith	3.64
1931	Johnny Allen	17	Johnny Allen	17-6	.739	Johnny Allen	3.02
	Guy Cantrell	17					
1930	Guy Cantrell	15	Guy Cantrell	15-5	.750	Guy Cantrell	2.68
	Hoot Gibson	15					
1929	Guy Cantrell	20	Phil Page	10-3	.769	Joe Samuels	2.65
1928	John Prudhomme	19	Rip Collins	17-9	.654	John Prudhomme	3.02
1927	Jim Faulkner	21	Jim Faulkner	21-10	.677	Jesse Doyle	2.82
1926	Owen Carroll	21	Owen Carroll	21-8	.724	Walter Stewart	2.99
1925	Myles Thomas	28	Myles Thomas	28-8	.778	WALTER STEWART	2.51
1924	Walter Stewart	24	Walter Stewart	24-11	.686	Walter Stewart	3.52
1923	Norman Glaser	16	Art Reynolds	11-5	.688	Billy Taylor	3.41
1922	Billy Taylor	18	Billy Taylor	18-15	.545	Stan Baumgartner	3.21
1921	Harry Thompson	15	Harry Thompson	15-9	.625	JOHN ENZMANN	2.25
	Bill Snyder	15					
1920	Pat Shea	27	Pat Shea	27-7	.794	Pat Shea	2.63

Year	Wins		Percentage			Earned Run Average	
1919	Wilbert Hubbell	17	Fred Hersche	16-5	.762	Wilbert Hubbell	1.91
	Hal Justin	17					
1918	Fred Hersche	21	Fred Hersche	21-6	.778	Fred Hersche	1.88
1917	HARRY THOMPSON	25	Bunny Hearn	23-9	.719	Bunny Hearn	2.03
1916	Bill McTigue	16	URBAN SHOCKER	15-3	.833	URBAN SHOCKER	1.31
	Ernie Herbert	16					
1915	Bill McTigue	17	Adolfo Luque	15-9	.625	(ERA not kept	
1914	Clint Rogge	17	Bull Wagner	13-7	.650	prior to 1916)	
1913	John Lush	17	John Lush	17-13	.567		
1912	Dick Rudolph	25	DICK RUDOLPH	25-10	.714		
1911	Dick Rudolph	18	Kid Mueller	17-8	.680		
	John Lush	18					
1910	Dick Rudolph	23	Dick Rudolph	23-15	.605		
1909	Dick Rudolph	23	Jim McGinley	22-13	.629		
1908	Dick Rudolph	18	Dick Rudolph	18-12	.600		
1907	Jim McGinley	22	Jim McGinley	22-10	.688		
1906	Jim McGinley	15	Jim McGinley	15-13	.536		
1905	Clarence Currie	16	Fred Falkenberg	11-10	.524		
1904	Clarence Currie	18	Clarence Currie	18-10	.643		
	Fred Falkenberg	18					
1903	Button Briggs	26	Button Briggs	26-8	.765		
1902	Button Briggs	20	LOUIE BRUCE	18-2	.900		
1901	Pop Williams	19	Pop Williams	19-13	.594		
1900	–		–				
1899	–		–				
1898	Kirtley Baker	17	Kirtley Baker	17-11	.607		
	Welcome Gaston	17					
1897	Bill Dinneen	21	Bill Dinneen	21-8	.724		
1896	–		–				
1895	–		–				
1890	John Coleman	11	John Coleman	11-4	.733		
1889	Tom Vickery	20	Bill Serad	19-16	.540		
1888	Albert Atkisson	33					
1887	Ned Crane	33	Ned Crane	33-13	.717		
1886	–						
1885	Jim McKinley	10	Jim McKinley	10-4	.714		
	Bill Stemmeyer	10					

League leaders capitalized

Toronto's Top Pitchers (most wins)

	Year	Wins	Losses	Pct.		Year	Wins	Losses	Pct.
Dick Rudolph	1907-1913	120	71	.628	Fred Herbert	1913-1916	48	50	.490
James McGinley	1906-1911	100	78	.562	Nick Strincevich	1942-1949	47	39	.547
Luke Hamlin	1933-1948	91	58	.611	Herb Briggs	1902-1903	46	16	.742
Jesse Doyle	1923-1928	73	55	.570	Sam Gibson	1925-1930	43	32	.573
Eddie Blake	1954-1959	67	54	.554	Claude Satterfield	1924-1928	40	27	.597
Guy Cantrell	1929-1932	66	48	.579	Clarence Fisher	1926-1930	39	34	.534
Walter Stewart	1924-1926	63	32	.663	Fred Hersche	1918-1919	37	11	.755
Don Johnson	1953-1959	62	51	.549	Pat Scantlebury	1958-1961	36	23	.610
Myles Thomas	1923-1925	57	27	.679	Louie Bruce	1902-1904	34	9	.791
Bunn Hearn	1913-1920	55	37	.598	Bob Tiefenauer	1957-1963	34	15	.694
Harry Thompson	1916-1922	54	33	.620	Bill McTigue	1915-1916	33	26	.559
Jack Crimian	1954-1959	53	28	.654	Wally Hilcher	1934-1935	32	22	.593
Steve Ridzik	1948-1963	53	44	.546	Bill Dinneen	1895-1897	32	24	.571
John Lush	1911-1913	52	34	.605	Bert Maxwell	1912-1913	32	28	.533
Frank Barnes	1929-1931	50	41	.549					

Toronto's Leading Hitters

Year	Batting		RBIs		Homers	
1967	John Ryan	.298	Tony Torchia	63	Sid O'Brien	10
1966	REG SMITH	.320	Tony Horton	85	Tony Horton	26
1965	JOE FOY	.302	Joe Foy	73	Joe Foy	14
					Jim Gosger	14
1964	Don Dillard	.288	Jim McKnight	89	Jim McKnight	24
1963	Lou Jackson	.315	Lou Jackson	89	Lou Jackson	31
1962	Neil Chrisley	.317	Steve Demeter	86	Steve Demeter	26
1961	Lou Johnson	.286	Steve Demeter	77	Steve Demeter	25
1960	Don Dillard	.294	Jim King	86	Jim King	24
1959	Archie Wilson	.294	Archie Wilson	100	Jim King	20
1958	ROCKY NELSON	.326	ROCKY NELSON	120	ROCKY NELSON	43
1957	Mike Goliat	.296	Rocky Nelson	102	Rocky Nelson	28
					Mike Goliat	28
1956	Archie Wilson	.301	Mike Goliat	86	Mike Goliat	23
1955	Archie Wilson	.319	Archie Wilson	119	Lou Limmer	17
1954	Elston Howard	.330	ED STEVENS	113	Ed Stevens	27
1953	Lew Morton	.307	Ed Stevens	92	Ed Stevens	19
					Mike Goliat	19
1952	Ferrell Anderson	.299	ED STEVENS	113	Ed Stevens	26
1951	Grover Bowers	.291	Les Fleming	79	Lew Morton	21
1950	John Mayo	.294	Bill Glynn	88	Bill Glynn	25
1949	John Welaj	.308	Ed Sanicki	102	Ed Sanicki	33
1948	John Welaj	.315	ED SANICKI	107	Ed Sanicki	21
					Hank Biasatti	21
1947	Ed Levy	.287	Ed Levy	71	Ed Levy	13
					Rollie Harrington	13
1946	Austin Knickerbocker	.294	Austin Knickerbocker	73	Austin Knickerbocker	12
1945	Ira Houck	.307	Ira Houck	75	James Pruett	8
1944	Tony Castano	.306	Herb Crompton	60	John Zontini	7
					James Tyack	7
1943	Harry Davis	.291	Harry Davis	64	Jim Ripple	8
1942	Frank Colman	.300	John Wyrostek	79	John Wyrostek	18
1941	Frank Colman	.295	Albert Rubeling	83	Albert Rubeling	14
1940	John Tyler	.288	Dario Lodigiani	78	Hubert Bates	8
					Emile De Jonghe	8
1939	Bob Elliott	.328	Emile De Jonghe	71	Jack Burns	11
1938	Ted Petoskey	.289	Frank Reiber	90	Frank Reiber	13
1937	Don Ross	.305	Ted Petoskey	74	Jim Walsh	15
1936	George McQuinn	.329	George McQuinn	61	George McQuinn	9
1935	Ike Boone	.350	Wes Schulmerich	106	Wes Schulmerich	17
1934	IKE BOONE	.372	Murray Howell	115	Joe Morrissey	8
					Ray Fitzgerald	8
1933	Ike Boone	.357	Ike Boone	103	Ike Boone	11
1932	John Rothrock	.327	Fred Henry	51	Murray Howell	6
					George Selkirk	6
1931	Ken Strong	.340	Ivy Shiver	89	Ivy Shiver	13
					Joe Rabbitt	13
1930	Joe Harris	.333	Joe Harris	82	Joe Harris	11
1929	Ralph Shinners	.337	Bill Sweeney	82	Joe Rabbitt	16
1928	DALE ALEXANDER	.380	DALE ALEXANDER	144	DALE ALEXANDER	31
1927	Dale Alexander	.338	Dale Alexander	98	Dale Alexander	12
					Bill Hargrave	12
1926	Bill Mullen	.357	Otis Miller	120	Cleo Carlyle	14
1925	Joe Kelly	.340	Joe Kelly	117	JOE KELLY	29

Year	Batting		RBIs		Homers	
1924	Joe Kelly	.351	Joe Kelly	117	Joe Kelly	24
1923	Red Wingo	.352	Joe Kelly	95	Red Wingo	20
1922	Eddie Onslow	.325	Red Wingo	122	RED WINGO	34
1921	Jesse Altenburg	.346			Eddie Onslow	12
					Andy Anderson	12
1920	Benny Kauff	.343			Benny Kauff	12
1919	Eddie Onslow	.303			George Whiteman	4
1918	Fred Lear	.345			FRED LEAR	5
1917	LARRY LAJOIE	.380			George Whiteman	7
1916	Dawson Graham	.294			Ray McKee	3
1915	Maurice Rath	.332			Gus Williams	8
1914	Robert Fisher	.311			Tim Jordan	13
1913	Joe Schultz	.299			Bill Bradley	4
					Bill O'Hara	4
1912	Benny Meyer	.343			TIM JORDAN	19
1911	Jack Slattery	.342			TIM JORDAN	20
1910	JACK SLATTERY	.310			ALBERT SHAW	11
1909	MYRON GRIMSHAW	.309			Ben Houser	6
1908	Bill Phyle	.271			BILL PHYLE	16
1907	JACK THONEY	.329			Jack Thoney	5
1906	JACK THONEY	.294			Jack Thoney	6
1905	Jack White	.277			JAMES MURRAY	9
1904	Jack White	.277			James Murray	4
1903	Louie Bruce	.356			Bill Massey	3
1902	Bill Massey	.313			Bill Massey	5
1901	Jim Bannon	.340			Frank Bonner	10
1900	Charley Carr	.327			–	
1899	JIM BANNON	.341			Romer Grey	7
1898	BUCK FREEMAN	.347			BUCK FREEMAN	23
1897	Buck Freeman	.357			BUCK FREEMAN	20
1896	Jimmy Casey	.329			Buck Freeman	7
1895	JUDSON SMITH	.373			JUDSON SMITH	14
1890	–				John Grim	1
					(First name unavailable) Ike	1
1889	William Hoover	.333			WILLIAM HOOVER	10
1888	Harry Decker	.313			–	
1887	NED CRANE	.428			–	
1886	JON MORRISON	.353			–	
1885	–				–	

League leaders capitalized

Toronto
Batting Champions

		Games	AB	Hits	Average			Games	AB	Hits	Average
1966	Reggie Smith	143	506	162	.320	1899	Jim Bannon	111	454	155	.341
1965	Joe Foy	140	500	151	.302	1898	Buck Freeman	122	496	172	.347
1958	Rocky Nelson	148	522	170	.326	1895	Judson Smith	113	466	174	.373
1934	Ike Boone	136	500	186	.372	1887	Ned Crane	97	376	161	.428
1928	Dale Alexander	169	621	236	.3800	1886	Jon Morrison	94	408	144	.353
1917	Napoleon Lajoie	151	581	221	.3803						
1910	Jack Slattery	100	365	113	.310						
1909	Myron Grimshaw	124	482	149	.309						
1907	Jack Thoney	102	413	136	.329						
1906	Jack Thoney	141	589	173	.294						

Toronto's Leading Hitters

(1,000 or more at bats)

	Games	AB	R	H	2B	3B	HR	RBI	SB	Average
Dale Alexander	322	1,178	198	424	75	22	43	241	19	.360
Ike Boone	494	1,694	291	581	99	26	29	318	15	.343
Buck Freeman	459	1,879	392	632	109	58	56	–	99	.336
Eddie Onslow	944	3,379	559	1,111	176	58	51	–	178	.329
Joe Kelly	548	2,208	376	722	107	33	90	329*	50	.327
Frank O'Rourke	402	1,639	333	530	112	21	17	–	63	.323
Murray Howell	327	1,154	160	366	73	28	18	220	13	.317
Jack Thoney	243	1,002	176	309	52	19	11	–	76	.308
George Whiteman	417	1,580	280	484	98	25	17	–	66	.306
Tim Jordan	653	2,291	403	262	121	28	55	–	101	.302
Otis Miller	487	1,689	248	501	78	13	11	–	32	.297
Rocky Nelson	357	1,288	232	379	60	13	82	253	5	.294
Archie Wilson	761	2,654	379	780	119	33	89	465	13	.294
Ted Petoskey	321	1,171	147	344	49	16	3	146	25	.294
Tommy Oliver	410	1,555	229	453	60	17	17	149	16	.291
Albert Shaw	419	1,526	282	442	74	23	42	–	96	.290
Harry Davis	722	2,312	346	661	129	21	28	270	50	.286
Lena Blackburne	583	2,093	259	595	84	25	9	–	94	.284
Bill Bradley	419	1,563	209	441	77	34	15	–	63	.282
Jack White	527	1,988	272	559	51*	31*	3*	–	119	.281
Sam Jethroe	636	2,281	412	639	101	24	73	277	101	.280
Eusebio Gonzales	681	2,290	396	640	96	22	1	–	169	.279
Nolen Richardson	701	2,658	317	741	123	18	9	273	57	.279
Joe Rabbitt	618	2,322	372	645	117	52	46	265	155	.278
Steve O'Neill	392	1,118	140	310	66	4	6	157	12	.277
Stan Johnson	349	1,300	170	360	40	13	12	96	17	.277
Loren Babe	528	1,893	282	523	82	16	39	222	18	.276
Hec Rodriguez	850	3,017	432	832	116	26	28	275	33	.276
Ed Stevens	667	2,367	368	651	94	20	100	432	19	.275
Mike Goliat	1,077	3,600	547	988	186	32	138	556	21	.274
Jim King	323	1,002	155	274	39	5	48	174	9	.273
Lew Morton	1,070	3,572	582	974	146	18	120	508	25	.273
Steve Demeter	440	1,511	190	395	69	9	68	256	5	.261
Ed Sanicki	407	1,400	231	341	46	6	64	251	10	.244
Sparky Anderson	485	1,608	209	389	48	12	10	106	20	.242
Lewis Carr	403	1,327	177	307	–	–	–	–	44	.231

– Incomplete.

Individual
Toronto
Records

Pitching

Wins – Cannonball Crane		33	1887
Albert Atkisson		33	1888
Wins (Career) – Dick Rudolph		120	
Percentage – Louie Bruce		.900	1902
Percentage (Career) – Louie Bruce		.791	
Strikeouts – Albert Atkisson		307	1888
Strikeouts (Game) – Ernie Broglio	v. Buffalo	15	1958
Most Wins In a Row – Cannonball Crane		16	1887
Lowest ERA – Urban Shocker		1.31	1916
Consecutive runless innings – Urban Shocker		54	1916

Hitting

Average (Prior to 1900) – Cannonball Crane	.428	1887
Average (Modern Era) – Napoleon Lajoie	.380	1917
Average (Career – 1,500 at bats) – Ike Boone	.343	
Home Runs – Rocky Nelson	43	1958
Home Runs (Career) – Mike Goliat	138	
Triples – Dan McGann	22	1897
Triples (Career) – Eddie Onslow, Buck Freeman	58	
Doubles – Dale Alexander	49	1928
Doubles (Career) – Mike Goliat	186	
RBIs – Dale Alexander	144	1928
RBIs (Career) – Mike Goliat	556	
Hits (Career) – Eddie Onslow	1,111	
Hits – Dale Alexander	236	1928
Runs (Prior to 1900) – Mike Slattery	134	1887
Runs (Modern era) – Frank O'Rourke	130	1920
Runs (Career) – Lew Morton	582	
Stolen Bases (Prior to 1900) – Mike Slattery	112	1887
Stolen Bases (Modern era) – Eusebio Gonzales	60	1921
Stolen Bases (Career – Prior to 1900) – Eddie Burke	204	
Stolen Bases (Career – Modern era) – Eddie Onslow	178	
Games (Career) – Mike Goliat	1,077	
At Bats (Career) – Mike Goliat	3,600	
Bases On Balls – Harry Davis	160	1945
Winning Streak	19	1925
Losing Streak	14	1932
Largest Winning score (v. Toledo)	36-5	1889
Largest Losing score (v. Atlanta)	20-0	1965

Bob Emslie   **Tip O'Neill**   **Arthur Irwin**

A dozen maidens in flowing robes saluted the Woodstock Wonder

Jenkins the greatest? How about the Doctor from Brandon!

Three of the most prominent Canadians in the major leagues prior to the turn of the century. O'Neill, the Woodstock Wonder, was the darling of the female fans and set a batting record which still exists. Emslie won 32 games for the Orioles before a lengthy career as an umpire and Ol' Foxy Irwin was the most versatile character in baseball. He was a manager, owner, inventor, model and author.

Does William Henry Watkins' name sound familiar?

How about Arthur (Cutrate) Irwin, Russell (Doctor) Ford or Robert (The Wig) Emslie?

Or even Nig Clarke, Tip O'Neill and Moony Gibson. We could also add a few more unfamiliar individuals in Jack Graney, Bill Phillips and Tom Gillean.

Ferguson Jenkins and about 120 other men can be added to this list of Canadian-born players who have either played, managed or umpired in the major leagues.

One managed six big league clubs. Another perfected the infielder's glove. A third, a tall, handsome fellow, was greeted every time he came to bat in St. Louis by a dozen maidens in flowing robes who sounded a fanfare on silver trumpets. That was the type of adulation Edward (Tip) O'Neill, from Woodstock, Ont., received the season he hit an incredible .492, the highest batting average in the history of major league baseball.

The year was 1887. Officials that season experimented with a rule that counted bases on balls as hits. But even without that help O'Neill's batting average would be four points greater than the next highest mark, the .438 hit in 1894 by Hugh Duffy of the Boston Nationals (who 26 years later managed Toronto).

That 1887 season was the first year a hitter could no longer call for a high or low pitch. Five balls constituted a walk and four strikes a strikeout.

O'Neill was credited with attracting the largest proportion of women fans of any player in the league. He cavorted against the gaudiest background baseball ever witnessed.

The Browns of the 1880s were owned by Chris Von der Ahe, a short, fat, uninhibited saloonkeeper who provided the customers with a spectacle that was part German beer garden, part Roman pageant and part American baseball.

Browns played their home games to the accompaniment of loud music rendered by Professor Poffenberger's German brass band and the competing cries of walrus-mustachioed beer waiters who peddled foaming steins of Von der Ahe's products throughout the stands.

After the games Von der Ahe trundled a wheelbarrow loaded with the day's receipts through the streets to the bank. But after a time the Browns and O'Neill attracted so many customers that Von der Ahe had to substitute a horse-drawn carriage. The wheelbarrow could not contain the cash.

The Browns won the title four years running. O'Neill in 1887 and '88 was the league batting and home run king, scoring a record 166 runs and 277 hits (including walks) in his big year.

To celebrate the 1888 series against New York, Von der Ahe outdid himself. He spent $20,000 to hire a special train to transport the Browns, hundreds of their fans, and a caboose loaded with beer to New York. The train was draped with banners and decorations and featured a huge canvas bearing a four-color

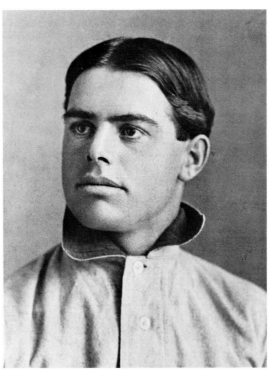

Far left: John Irwin, an infielder, wasn't as famous as his older brother Arthur.

Left: A young George (Moony) Gibson, "the Iron Backstop" of the Pittsburgh Pirates. He played 1,213 games.

Below: Moony Gibson (middle) reminiscing in 1951 with oldtimers Tris Speaker, right, and Hank Gowdy in London's Labatt's Park. Gowdy holds ball Speaker hit into stands in a 1912 exhibition game in London.

portrait of a triumphantly nonchalant Tip O'Neill. A large caption proclaimed him "Batting Champion of the World."

O'Neill hit .337 in 1889 and then took part in a players' strike. Led by another Canadian baseball star, Arthur (Cutrate) Irwin of Toronto, more than half the major league players signed a declaration of independence from the National League and American Association.

Principal complaint of the players was the $2,500 salary limit. They formed the Players' League (The Brotherhood) in the major cities. O'Neill joined Charles Comiskey's Chicago team.

The new league folded after a year and O'Neill returned to St. Louis, but Von der Ahe never forgave his striking players and sent O'Neill to Cincinnati. For the first time since giving up pitching to play the outfield the Woodstock Wonder hit under .300 and he quit ball the next year. He operated a tavern in Montreal until his death in 1915.

O'Neill's big year, 1887, was also the season that William Henry Watkins, a 28-year-old from Brantford, managed his Detroit Nationals to the league championship over Harry Wright's Philadelphia team and the Chicago White Stockings of the famed Cap Anson.

Wright was even more prominent. He later would be termed "The Father of Professional Baseball" because he organized and managed the first pro team, the undefeated Cincinnati Red Stockings of 1869.

Watkins, the young manager from Brantford, had a team loaded with Hall of Famers Dan Brouthers and Sam Thompson as well as Ned Hanlon, Sure Shot Dunlap, Jack Rowe, Hardy Richardson and Pretzels Getzein, who won 29 games that year.

In the world championships Watkins' Detroit team beat Comiskey's St. Louis (AA) club 10-5 in a 15-game tour of 10 cities. The Woodstock Wonder was with that St. Louis team.

Watkins, a manager at the age of 24 with Indianapolis, also handled the Kansas City and Pittsburgh teams before retiring in 1899 at 40.

Cutrate Irwin, whose brother John was also a major league player, was the busiest and most versatile character in the game for almost 40 years. No man played so many roles, both on the field and behind the scenes.

His tendency to jump from job to job explains his nickname – Cutrate. His colleagues maintained he had a compulsion to take new jobs and when a managerial post was open he would offer to take it at less pay than other applicants.

Irwin was author of a book, "Practical Ballplaying", and captain of the Phillies of the 1880s. The book explained positioning for double plays, fielding certain hitters, bunting, base stealing, running, anticipation of hitters and everything that was scientific rather than just chance.

He also posed as a photographer's model to illustrate various fielding positions, batting stances and plays in action.

Also known as Foxy, Doc and Artful Dodger, Irwin played shortstop for 13 seasons and participated in 1,001 games. But Irwin's most lasting contribution to baseball was his padded glove invention. Until 1884, with the exception of one player who briefly used a kid glove in the field, baseball was played barehanded.

That year Irwin was the shortstop, captain and key man of the NL's Providence Grays. Late in the season, when the Grays were engaged in a close race for the pennant with Boston, Irwin broke two fingers of his left hand while fielding a hard-hit ball.

Today this would put a player out of action for several weeks, but Irwin persuaded manager Frank Bancroft that he could still play. He bought a buckskin glove several sizes too large, padded it and sewed the bandages of his two broken fingers together so they would fit snugly into one of the glove's roomy fingers.

His first appearance on the field wearing a glove created a stir among fans. There were some cries of "sissy." But Irwin fielded and helped lead the Grays to the pennant and to a sweep of the championship series against the New York Metropolitans.

During his career Irwin managed Washington, Philadelphia, New York and Boston and umpired for two years in the National League.

Irwin made enough money in baseball to buy one team, the Kansas City Blues, and to become part owner of his home-town Toronto Maple Leafs. He also managed the Leafs on two different occasions.

Irwin used to waggle his hand with his two crooked fingers, which had never knit properly, and talk about how he came to invent the baseball glove. He died in 1921.

So little has been written about Canadians in the major leagues that when George (Moony) Gibson of London, Ont., died in 1967 the Canadian Press in its obituary said that Gibson was the only Canadian to ever manage a major league team.

He was the third. A robust, durable farm boy, Gibson played in the majors from 1906 to 1918 and played in 1,213 games. He was the "iron backstop" and in '09 caught 157 of the Pittsburgh Pirates' 159 games.

He is considered one of Pittsburgh's great catchers. Gibson possessed a remarkable, accurate throwing arm and was superb at developing young pitchers, notably Babe Adams, the only rookie to win three successive World Series games.

Gibson wasn't a .300 hitter but was dangerous when a run was needed to tie or win a game.

After concluding his career with the Giants in 1918, Gibson came to Toronto to manage the Leafs and then returned to the majors for 14 years. He managed the Pirates and Cubs, coached Washington Senators, and spent some time as a Pirate scout. The Pirates he managed in the '20s were a collection of clowns, carousers and hell-raisers. But talented. They were known as "Gibson's Follies" and included Rabbit Maranville, Charlie Grimm, Possum Whitted, Pie Traynor, Max Carey, Nig Clarke, Mule Watson, Kiki Cuyler and Chief Moses Yellowhorse, a fullblooded Pawnee Indian, whose hobby was biting the necks off whisky bottles.

Nig Clarke, who played briefly for Gibson, was a young catcher from Amherstburg, Ont. He had an unbelievable afternoon in 1902 in the Texas League when he hit eight homers in one game – eight-for-eight.

The lefthanded slugger had already hit four over the fence for Corsicana against Texarkana when he came to bat for the fifth time in the game.

A cattleman shouted, "Hit another homer,

Nig, and I'll give you $50." Clarke socked it out. When he came out the next time a rival cattleman rushed onto the field waving a $100 bill. Nig promptly belted number six.

To the astonishment of everyone he added number seven and when he came up for the eighth time the fans began to chant and wave money. Number eight disappeared over the fence. Afterwards the fans surrounded Nig and showered him with money. He had knocked in 16 runs in the 51-3 win. A hat was passed and over $500 was collected. Local merchants gave him dozens of suits, shoes, socks, shirts, ties and sets of underwear.

In the majors from 1905 to 1920, mainly with Cleveland, Nig hit only six homers in 1,536 at bats in 506 games. He had a lifetime batting average of .254.

Until Fergy Jenkins came out of Chatham to establish himself as one of baseball's great righthanders with his blazing fastball and excellent control, undoubtedly the greatest Canadian to pitch in the big leagues was Russell (Doctor) Ford, a farm boy from Brandon, Man.

No rookie has ever broken into the majors quite the way Ford did in 1910 with the New York Yankees. He won 26 games against just six losses and compiled eight shutouts in posting a remarkable 1.65 earned run average.

Ford went the distance 29 times in 33 starts and pitched 300 innings for the second place New York team.

Ford's key to success was a strip of emery paper wrapped around a ring and exposed by a small hole cut in his glove. With this he scuffed the ball, which would do a series of weird dips, jumps and swerves after being released.

Spalding's "Baseball Guide of 1911" commented that it was a "sheer waste of time for a batter to expect to get a safe hit off the sensational Canadian."

He won 22 games in 1911. When he started off his third season with a string of wins, sports writers started comparing Ford with the great Christy Mathewson. Besides his "emery" ball he had a dancing knuckleball and a blazing fastball. But Ford suddenly lost his effectiveness. Perhaps it was because the Yanks were a last place team that year.

One uncorroborated story has it that in

Dublin-born Jimmy Archer graduated from Toronto sandlots to a lengthy major league catching career with the Chicago Cubs. Inset is Russell (Doctor) Ford, the Brandon farm boy who perfected "emery ball" pitch and won 26 games as a rookie with Yankees.

1912 Ford fractured the skull of an opposing batter with an erratic "emery" pitch and that the player survived but never played again. Ford was said to be so unnerved by the incident that he abandoned his "emery" ball. Without his gimmick going for him Ford set a Yankee record for games lost – 21. After an 11-18 season with another poor New York team Ford jumped to the Federal League, a third major circuit formed by a group of wealthy industrialists.

He was a 21-game winner for Buffalo in his first season but lost nine of his 14 decisions in 1915 and when the league folded he also quit baseball with a record of 98 wins and 71 losses. Baseball's first great "emery" ball pitcher died at Rockingham, N.C., in 1960 at the age of 76.

First Canadian-born player in the majors was Bill Phillips of Saint John, N.B., a splendid fielding first baseman with Cleveland, Brooklyn and Kansas City. He played over 1,000 games, collected 1,130 hits and batted .322 for Brooklyn in 1887.

The Maritimes, like southwestern Ontario, produced an unusually high number of big league players. However, the London, Guelph, Chatham area was a particularly strong breeding ground for baseball, especially in the pre-1900s and early part of the century.

Guelph claimed the "world championship" around the time of the Civil War. The London Tecumsehs were the first minor league champions of North America in 1877 when its team finished a game ahead of Pittsburgh Alleghenys in the International Association. Guelph was also in that league along with Rochester, Manchester, N.H., Columbus and Lynn, Mass.

Other good major leaguers from the London area were pitcher Oscar Judd of Ingersoll, first basemen Tommy Burgess and Frank Colman of London, outfielders Bunky Congalton of Guelph and Jack Graney of St. Thomas.

Graney played 1,402 games for Cleveland from 1908-1922, and on retirement was the first player to become a baseball broadcaster. He did the play-by-play of Indians' games for years.

Earlier in his career Graney was involved in two "firsts." In 1914 he became the first player to face Boston Red Sox's rookie pitcher, Babe Ruth, and two years later (June 26, 1916) the Canadian-born left fielder was the first major league player to wear a number.

Graney wore a number, which was attached to the sleeve of his uniform.

Several Canadians have been prominent in the officiating end of the game, none more eminent than Robert (The Wig) Emslie of Guelph. He was a 32-game winner for Baltimore in 1884 before an arm injury caused his early retirement as a player.

He served baseball longer than any man except Connie Mack. Emslie was in baseball for 60 years, first as a player, then as an umpire for 33 years, and later as a member of NL's umpire's advisory board to scout and train new umpires.

Emslie and his fellow umpire, Bill Klem, are given much credit for improving the working conditions of umpires, raising them from ill-paid and despised minor functionaries to their present well-paid status.

When he started in 1891 only one umpire was used. He had to call foul lines, bases and watch for shenanigans players were always pulling on each other. In the early years Emslie had only a wooden shed in which to clean up after a game.

He had many famous run-ins with John McGraw of the Giants and along with Hank O'Day was involved in the famous Fred Merkle "bonehead" play of 1908, the incident which eventually cost the Giants the pennant to the Cubs.

Merkle was on first and Moose McCormick on third when Al Bridwell singled over second to score the tie-breaking run in the 1-1 game. Watching McCormick crossing the plate, the teen-age rookie pulled up short of the bag and headed for the dressing room while fans poured onto the field.

However, the alert Cubs spotted Merkle's lapse and grabbed a ball and stepped on second for a force out. Emslie and O'Day called Merkle out, nullifying McCormick's run. The umps, however, had to call the game a tie when the fans invaded the Polo Grounds field.

When the season finished in a tie the Cubs and Giants had to replay the game and the Cubs won.

McGraw was fond of referring to Emslie as "Blind Bob" and once told the newspapers that if an apple and orange were placed at second base Emslie, at home plate, couldn't tell which was which. When NL president Thomas Lynch ordered eye examinations, McGraw solemnly bade Emslie farewell. But "Blind Bob" at 52 turned out to have the keenest eyesight of all umpires.

Bald from an early age, Emslie wore a wig. One day John (Dirty Jack) Doyle attempted to rip it off after a decision went against his team. But Emslie, after a brawl, managed to keep his hairpiece.

McGraw once was fined $2,500 for proclaiming to 20,000 fans after a disputed Emslie decision, "Old Bob needs a hairpin for his wig!"

Besides Irwin and Emslie, another Canadian to umpire was Tom Gillean of London. He was the NL's first paid arbiter in 1879 and received $5 a game.

Bill (Sandy) Reid, of London, Win Kellum of Waterford and Paul Runge of St. Catharines also umpired in the major leagues.

Many Canadians have been in the majors for only a game or two. But there have been countless good ones. Fort William's Jeff Heath was a powerful hitter for Cleveland who twice made the all-star team and led the league in triples. Hamilton's Frank O'Rourke, an infielder, played more than 1,100 games. Toronto's Goody Rosen was an all-star in 1945 for the Dodgers when he hit .326. Pitchers included Joe Krakauskas of Montreal and Hamilton, Phil Marchildon of Penetanguishene and Dick Fowler, Toronto, the only Canadian to pitch a major-league no-hitter.

Fowler also pitched a 16-inning game against St. Louis before losing 1-0 in 1942. After the war he returned to the Philadelphia A's. His lone win that season came when the tall righthander beat the Browns 1-0 on a no-hitter on September 9.

In recent years most Canadians to make the big leagues have been pitchers with the exception of Montreal's Pete Ward and Tim Harkness. The better pitchers have been Ted Bowsfield from British Columbia, Claude Raymond of St. Jean, Que., and Toronto's Ron Taylor, who sparkled in two World Series for the Cardinals and Mets in the 1960s. He didn't allow a hit in either series in four relief appearances.

At present the dominant Canadians on major league rosters are Jenkins; John Hiller (Toronto) with Detroit; and Reggie Cleveland of Swift Current, who is with the Red Sox.

Jenkins, who seven times has won 20 or more games in a season, has pitched for Philadelphia, Chicago, Texas and Boston and in 1977 ranks 15th on the list of greatest strikeout pitchers. He began the season with 2,344, which puts him ahead of company that includes Lefty Grove, Rube Waddell, Early Wynn and Eddie Plank; and about to pass Sandy Koufax, Robin Roberts and Sam McDowell. Jenkins has a won-loss career mark of 203-150.

Hiller is one of the best relief pitchers in the majors. He has a record of 65-51 in 395 games and Cleveland is 75-73 in 229 games.

One Canadian with a good chance of cracking the Blue Jays' lineup this year is Vancouver's Dave McKay, a third baseman. He hit a homer in his first major league at bat with Minnesota in 1975 and was drafted off the Twins' roster last November in the expansion draft.

Joe Krakauskas had a blazing fastball for Washington but usually walked more batters than he struck out. Inset is hard-hitting Frank Colman, a first baseman-outfielder from London, Ont.

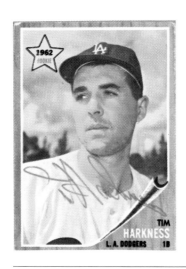
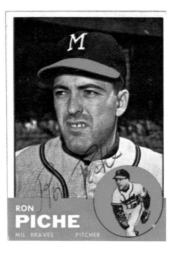

TIM
HARKNESS
L. A. DODGERS 1B

RON
PICHE
MIL BRAVES PITCHER

PITCHER
CLAUDE RAYMOND

CARDINALS

RON TAYLOR pitcher

The pride of Swift Current, Sask., Reggie Cleveland of the Red Sox.

Scarboro's John Hiller, one of the premier relief pitchers in majors.

166

Only 14 pitchers have struck out more men than Ferguson Jenkins. The Chatham, Ont., hurler ranks among the greats in baseball.

The American League: from Ban to MacPhail and The Babe, Ty, Foxx

The league that flirted with Toronto in 1899 finally popped the question in 1976

In 1899 there were reports circulating in baseball circles that Byron Bancroft (Ban) Johnson was eyeing Toronto as a possible member of his highly successful Western League.

Johnson believed America was ready for another major league and he had many receptive listeners among the players. Another league would give them some bargaining power.

Within a year the former Cincinnati sports editor renamed his organization the American League. In 1901 Johnson declared war on the established National League and began raiding the rosters of the "senior" circuit. That boldness was the start of the illustrious history of the American League, which now comes, warmly welcomed, to the city with which it flirted 77 years earlier.

The Blue Jays have become members of a proud organization which has boasted the greatest players the game has produced–Babe Ruth, Ty Cobb, Walter Johnson, Lefty Grove, Ted Williams, Lou Gehrig, George Sisler, Tris Speaker, Jimmy Foxx, Joe DiMaggio and Mickey Mantle–as well as baseball's most renowned teams–the Yankees, Athletics, Red Sox, Tigers, White Sox and Orioles.

Despite New York's loss to the Cincinnati Reds last fall, the "junior" circuit still has won 43 of the 73 World Series the two leagues have contested since 1903.

But let's go back to the turn of the century and the founding of the upstart American League. Johnson and his associate from Chi-cago, Charles A. Comiskey, had been aiming that way for years.

In 1893 they had revived the Western League, a dormant minor league circuit that included such solid baseball cities as Minneapolis, Milwaukee, Kansas City and Toledo. Gradually they raised the level of play. In two years they had made the league the strongest of the minors.

Johnson accomplished this feat by arranging for solid ownership of each of his franchises and by strongly backing his umpires in all disputes, thus assuring the fans that orderly games would be played.

Things were different in the National League. The arbiters were a sorry lot, largely because no man with any backbone could put up with the threats, insults and physical violence an umpire had to endure from fans and players, or with the open disdain from club owners.

NL club owners took pains to bar from their parks any umpire whose work had displeased them. In Cincinnati and New York the owners would simply insist that this or that man, be he Honest John Kelly or doubtful Jack Kerins, could not officiate at any game their clubs were involved in.

Should a manager or owner take sudden offense at an umpire assigned to his club he might chase the man out and assign a player to decide the outs and call the balls and strikes.

Johnson promised himself that if he did nothing else he would put iron in the authority of his umpires.

Byron Bancroft (Ban) Johnson, founder of American League in 1900 and Leland S. (Lee) MacPhail Jr., American League President since 1974.

Charles Comiskey of Chicago, a founding father of American League.

Feuds with Ban Johnson drove John McGraw to National League in 1902.

Two of baseball's great pitchers—Walter (The Big Train) Johnson and Clark (Old Fox) Griffith pose before Washington Senators' opener in 1930.

By 1896 the wheels in Johnson's head were turning. If the NL dropped any of its 12 franchises, he would replace it with a Western League team. In 1900 the NL cut back to eight teams. Johnson moved into Chicago and Cleveland. His task was made easier by discontent among NL players. Many were left without jobs or wound up in the minors when the league dropped four clubs.

The players resented the high-handed methods of the owners, the National Agreement which contained a Reserve Clause, and the fact that they could be traded anywhere. Even those still with jobs feared massive pay cuts. To combat all this they formed the Professional Baseball Players' Protective Association.

Meanwhile, Johnson was expanding eastward. He attracted owners in Baltimore, Washington, Philadelphia and Boston to go along with teams already in Detroit, Chicago, Cleveland and Milwaukee.

To obtain players the new league raided the senior loop's rosters for stars as well as everyday players. Large salaries were offered. Johnson realized that many of these players were prepared to break their contracts because the owners had turned down some modest requests from the players' protective association.

Also prior to the 1901 season the Johnson league announced it no longer honored the National Agreement, which had made the AL a minor league, and would ignore the Reserve Clause.

Biggest catch of the new league was Nap Lajoie, who would eventually wind up in Toronto to manage a pennant winning team in 1917. Lajoie was persuaded to move from the Phillies to the Athletics for a three-year contract of $24,000. Most players were making between $2,000 and $3,000 a season.

A lawsuit immediately followed. By 1902 an injunction was obtained preventing Lajoie from playing, but in Philadelphia only. He was quickly sold to Cleveland and when that club played in Philadelphia, Lajoie took a vacation on the beach at Atlantic City, N.J.

Other future Hall of Famers to join the new league were Jimmy Collins, Hugh Duffy (who

Baseball's greatest hitter, the Georgia Peach–Ty Cobb.

171

Above: Cleveland's "Big Four": From left–Mike Garcia, Bob Lemon, Early Wynn and Bob Feller. They won 79 games in 1951.

Right: Virgil (Fire) Trucks on his way to first of two no-hitters he hurled for Detroit in 1952.

Satchel Paige was 42 and long time star of Negro leagues before getting his chance in major leagues. Helped Indians win 1948 pennant. At 46 he became oldest man to pitch shutout, a 12-inning 1-0 win.

also later would manage in Toronto), Connie Mack, McGraw, Cy Young, Roger Bresnahan, Clark Griffith, Wilbert Robinson and Joe McGinnity. Of the 185 players who appeared that season, 111 had previous experience in the NL, though all were not necessarily jumpers.

A 140-game schedule was drawn up for the 1901 season and rosters were limited to 14 men. Opening day was April 24 but because of rain only one game, between Cleveland and Chicago, which would win the pennant, was played.

In the first season of Johnson's new league the champion White Sox were led by their pitcher-manager Clark Griffith, who won 24 games, Nixey Callahan, Billy Sullivan, Roy Patterson, Fielder Jones and Dummy Hoy.

The Boston club, which has been variously recorded as the Puritans, Pilgrims and Somersets (after owner Charles Somers) started strong but ended in second place. Boston had a great collection of stars led by manager Jimmy Collins and ex-Toronto slugging star Buck Freeman, who hit .346, 12 homers and 15 triples.

The immortal Cy Young, on the mound,

won 33 of the 511 games he was to win. Ex-Toronto player George Stallings, who would later gain fame as manager of the 1914 "Miracle Braves" of Boston, led the Detroit team into third ahead of Mack's A's.

The league that year had many players who had jumped up from Toronto's minor league team or who would later play for Toronto–Freeman, Jack Slattery, Tim Jordan, Albert Shaw, Bill Crystall, Fred Mitchell, Doc Casey, Charlie Carr, Bill Bradley and Jack Dunn.

Detroit opened its first AL season against the Milwaukee Brewers with a rookie on the mound–Roscoe Miller, who won 23 games that year and then never won more than seven in a season. Trailing 13-4 in the last of the ninth the Tigers scored 10 times to win 14-13. This set the pattern for the Brewers' initial season. (They were replaced by St. Louis the following year and didn't return to the AL until 1970).

Detroit in 1901 had two of the scrappiest players in the game in its infield–Kid Gleason and Kid Elberfield.

In Philadelphia the graceful 6 feet 1 inch, 200 pound Lajoie played second and was the

Yankee teammates mob Mickey Mantle after his ninth inning grand-slam homer in Chicago.

Ted Williams' homer against Washington fails to enthuse Red Sox teammate Dick Gernert.

Joltin' Joe DiMaggio is greeted by Joe Collins (left), Yogi Berra and batboy after homer.

hero of the Quaker City as he hit .422. (That's still an AL mark, but foul balls weren't counted as strikes that year). He led in homers and runs batted in. (RBIs did not become a part of the official averages until many years later.)

The A's star pitchers were Chuck Fraser and a rookie southpaw – Eddie Plank. A Hall of Famer later, Plank won 325 in his career.

John McGraw's Orioles finished fifth even though the entire infield batted over .300. This batting feat has never been duplicated in the history of the league. Catcher Bresnahan was a super athlete who played the outfield, infield and even pitched in two games.

Known as the Duke of Tralee, Bresnahan was the first to wear shin guards and even tried a batting helmet following a bean ball accident. Joe McGinnity won 26 games with a smooth, effortless underhand motion that resulted in a natural curve. He became known as Iron Man McGinnity because he often pitched both ends of a doubleheader.

Earl Moore of Cleveland pitched the league's first no-hitter against Chicago only to lose it in the 11th. The Brewers had a pitcher, Pete Dowling, who lost 27 games. It was that kind of year for the Brewers.

The league in 1901 abounded in colorful nicknames – Boileryard Clarke, Tacks Latimer, ZaZa Harvey, Socks Seybold, Crazy Schmidt, Nig Cuppy, Ducky Holmes and Snake Wiltse.

Washington finished sixth that first AL year, Cleveland Blues seventh and Milwaukee, 35 ½ games out, last.

The following year Johnson and McGraw were continually at odds with each other. The fiery McGraw was suspended in July and immediately began making plans to join the rival National League.

He prompted Baltimore owners to sell the club to John T. Brush, chairman of the NL's executive committee. Brush proceeded to sell off all the top Orioles to his league. When the Orioles were unable to field a team on July 17 Johnson revoked the franchise from Brush. Johnson took it over and arranged for every club to contribute players to stock the sabotaged team. The Orioles operated on league funds the remainder of the season but it was a triumph for the AL.

Connie Mack, the scorecard-waving bench manager of the Philadelphia A's. Managed 53 years, winning nine pennants and five world titles.

In one of Bill Veeck's many stunts with St. Louis Browns, he employed baseball's only 43-inch pinch-hitter, Eddie Gaedel, who walked in only appearance against Tigers. He batted for lanky Frank Saucier in 1951 game. Gaedel sits between Matt Batts (left) and Jim McDonald.

They loved Casey Stengel everywhere he went, but especially in his home town–Kansas City.

By 1902 the American League was outdrawing the opposition. The following year an agreement was signed, calling both leagues equal (a fact McGraw disagreed with for years). There was no World Series in 1904 because McGraw still refused to recognize the AL as anything but an "upstart league."

Declaration of peace before the 1903 season cost the AL players their right to prevent owners from trading them whenever they chose.

Johnson invaded New York in 1903 and the success of the new AL club removed any doubt of the major league status of the circuit as the Highlanders (also the Porchclimbers but later the Yankees) competed against the Giants and Superbas (later the Robins and Dodgers) for fans.

177

Playing in freshly opened Highlander Park in upper Manhattan, the new club in town got away to a slow start but rallied to finish fourth with a squad which included Willie Keeler, Jack Chesbro and Clark Griffith. The club planted a seed which would bloom into baseball's most successful franchise, the Yankees.

In the league's first 19 years the A's, White Sox, Tigers and Red Sox took turns winning the pennant. Then the Bambino, Babe Ruth, landed in New York and baseball's greatest dynasty was launched.

From 1921 until 1964 the Yankees of Miller Huggins, Joe McCarthy, Bucky Harris, Casey Stengel, Ralph Houk and Yogi Berra won 29 pennants and 20 World Series titles.

Johnson, after 26 years of distinguished service, resigned as the league's head in 1927 because of ill health. Ernest S. Barnard held the post until his death in 1931 and William Harridge then took over for 28 years, resigning in 1959.

During the Harridge tenure the Browns moved from St. Louis to Baltimore in 1954. In 1955 the A's left Philadelphia in favor of Kansas City. Joe Cronin's presidency lasted until 1973, a period of baseball's greatest overhaul. In 1961 the AL expanded, putting teams into Los Angeles (later Anaheim) and Washington while the Senators moved to Minnesota to become the Twins.

In 1968 the A's again moved, this time to Oakland. The following year the AL again expanded, this time into Kansas City and Seattle. A year later the Seattle franchise moved to Milwaukee. The last franchise shift came in 1972 when Washington moved to Texas.

Playoffs were introduced in 1969 with the innovation of divisional play. In 1972 the league adopted the revolutionary "designated hitter" rule, which allows an assigned hitter for the pitcher.

The present league president is Leland S. MacPhail Jr., who in 1942, at 24, was the youngest general manager in the history of the International League. His team was Toronto.

Progress since the league began in 1901?

That year it attracted 1,683,584 fans. In 1976 attendance was a record 14,657,802, an exciting prospect for the two new teams – Blue Jays and the Seattle Mariners.

The greatest attraction in baseball in 1976 was Detroit's Mark (The Bird) Fidrych.

Southpaw Paul Splittorff beat Yankees in playoffs. Leads all Kansas City Royals' pitchers in wins.

Ferguson Jenkins, a 25-game winner for Texas in his
first year in American League.

George Brett, Kansas City
Royals' batting champion.

The swift Ralph Garr, a
.300 hitter for White Sox.

Veteran Willie Horton,
Detroit's designated hitter.

Hard-hitting Lee May,
led league in RBIs for Orioles.

Rod Carew, Minnesota
Twins' all-star infielder.

First baseman Mike Hargrove,
Texas Rangers' top hitter.

Jim (Catfish) Hunter pitched
299 innings for New York.

Hal McRae, league's top DH
for Kansas City Royals.

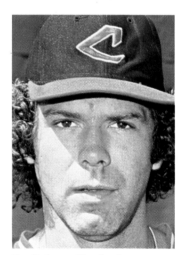

Pat Dobson, Cleveland
Indians' 16-game winner.

Shortstop Toby Harrah
hit 15 home runs for Rangers.

Sixto Lezcano, Brewers'
versatile outfielder.

Third baseman Don Money
of Milwaukee Brewers.

180

Catcher Thurman Munson,
MVP for New York Yankees.

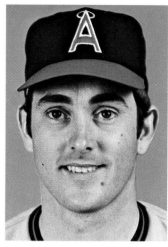

Nolan Ryan, strikeout king
of the California Angels.

Veteran pitcher Luis Tiant
won 21 games for Red Sox.

Wilbur Wood of White Sox
is ace of pitching staff.

Jim Palmer, Cy Young Award
winner for Baltimore.

Outfielder Rusty Staub,
Detroit's clutch hitter.

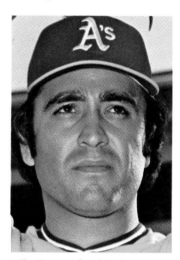

Mike Torrez of Oakland
had a low 2.50 ERA in 1976.

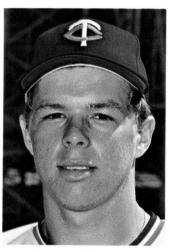

Butch Wynegar, Minnesota's
outstanding young catcher.

Veteran John (Boog) Powell,
Cleveland Indians' slugger.

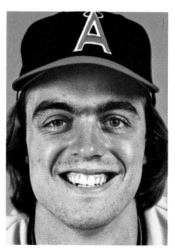

Fireballer Frank Tanana
won 19 games for California.

Claudell Washington stole
37 bases for Oakland Athletics.

Carl Yastrzemski of Boston
hit 21 HRs and had 102 RBIs.

The Blue Jays: Toronto's impossible dream a reality after 90 years

A franchise after frustration and rejection for Labatt's, Webster and the CIBC

It is probably a good thing Toronto politicians and businessmen ignored Albert Goodwill Spalding's advice in 1886.

If they had heeded the suggestion of one of baseball's eminent pioneers we now wouldn't be sitting in on a significant moment in the city's history...the arrival of major league ball and the debut of the Blue Jays.

Spalding was always eager to encourage the growth of baseball. He took touring teams on global tours of Europe, Asia and Australia in the 1880s.

Perhaps he was anxious to broaden the base of his baseball equipment empire, when, on a visit to Toronto in the winter of 1886, Spalding suggested that Toronto should apply for a franchise in the National League.

Maybe Sir John A. Macdonald would have thrown out the first ball. Ever since that day this city has been wanting to get into the big leagues.

Sporting Life in 1890 said, "The day will come when Canada will have a professional league of its own and there will be an interesting contest for the Canadian championship followed by a series for the championship of America. Be patient, Canadian ball tossers, the time for all this is in the near future."

Toronto was mentioned in 1899 when Ban Johnson was scouting cities to put franchises in for his fledgling American League. In 1919 there were reports that Toronto would be part of another major league – the New Liberty League. The writer described the International League as a "cheese circuit" and said that Toronto was tired of "being the truck horse for a lot of ham cities."

A couple of years later another newspaper story said that "Toronto...is regarded as the finest (city) in minor league baseball and if there was ever a vacancy in the 'big leagues' the Queen City would be the likely choice."

In 1926 when Toronto built its large, modern stadium talk of the majors again popped up: "Today we find fans and promoters talking of the possibility of securing a major league franchise...Toronto is ready to step into the 'big time'." Rarely did a year pass after that in which Toronto was not mentioned as a major-league possibility, especially when a franchise in financial straits was looking for a likely home. But it just never happened.

However, in 1973 talk of expanding the facilities at the Canadian National Exhibition Stadium brought forth several groups anxious to pursue either an expansion franchise or an existing club eager to move.

During an Argonaut football game at the CNE that fall two influential politicians, Premier William Davis of the province and Metro Chairman Paul Godfrey, agreed on the "benefits, need and wisdom" of expanding the stadium to attract major league ball.

It was now only a matter of time and dollars – some of it public and the rest corporate.

Baseball wanted Toronto; but a stadium had never been available to seat big league crowds.

Joe Cronin, Hall of Famer and Chairman of the American League, presents membership certificate to Blue Jays' chairman of the board, Howard Webster (middle) and executive vice-president Peter Bavasi at expansion draft meetings in New York.

Metro Chairman Paul Godfrey was forefront among civic politicians who fought for a baseball franchise.

At 36 the youngest president in Labatt's history, Donald McDougall was the driving force behind Toronto's previously impossible dream—a major league franchise.

In the ensuing months, following the conversation of Premier Davis and Godfrey, the necessary steps were taken to commit the provincial and Metro governments to a renovated and expanded stadium which would seat more than 50,000. The baseball stadium would accommodate approximately 40,000.

About this time a significant happening was the promotion of D. J. (Don) McDougall to president of Labatt Breweries of Canada Ltd. He was 36, youngest president in the company's history.

McDougall was a native of Prince Edward Island, a proud "down-homer" and an avid baseball fan. During the next three years, until a franchise was finally obtained, McDougall was the driving force behind Toronto's previously impossible dream.

The hunt was filled with immense frustrations, particularly during the "San Francisco period" when Labatt's tried to buy the NL Giants. Court hearings followed, injunctions, restraining orders and finally disappointment when two men promised to put up enough money ($8 million) to keep the Giants on the west coast.

The scene in the Plaza Hotel's Terrace Room in New York as Toronto and Seattle officials select 30 players each in the expansion draft. Screen right flashed name and statistics of each player drafted.

Toronto's first choice was shortstop Robert M. Bailor of the Baltimore Orioles. Vice-president and general manager Peter Bavasi holds card.

Far left: Danny Kaye, movie actor and entertainer as well as part-owner of the Seattle Mariners, announces name of first player selected – Ruppert Jones.

The battle was costly. Not only in man hours but financially. It cost McDougall's firm and his equal partner, R. Howard Webster, chairman and president of The Globe and Mail and Vulcan Assets Dominion Ltd., along with the Canadian Imperial Bank of Commerce (a 10 percent partner), $250,000. That was the time, McDougall said, "to sit back and think."

Chairman Godfrey found himself in a tense situation. "The political wolves were at my door. I had rebuilt a stadium with taxpayers' money and had no tenant."

But, dramatically, Toronto got back into the baseball picture three weeks later. The American League voted 11-1 to expand to 14 teams in 1977 with Seattle and Toronto getting franchises – for $7 million each.

Then baseball commissioner Bowie Kuhn attempted to force the AL to put a team into Washington first, to honor a prior commitment to the U.S. capital. Kuhn's power play failed when the AL ignored his wishes. When the National League could not agree on expanding into Toronto and Washington for 1977 the long, tedious struggle was over, the American League had arrived, the Blue Jays were aloft.

Privately, negotiations and secret dealings began the summer of 1974. Labatt's was interested. After preliminary discussions with Kuhn, Chub Feeney, president of the NL, and Lee MacPhail of the AL, the company decided to pursue baseball for Toronto.

"Pursue" was an understatement. For the next 24 months there wasn't a baseball meeting, World Series game or all-star contest without the attendance of McDougall or other Labatt's officials, along with Chairman Godfrey and civic officials.

But there were other Toronto groups interested in acquiring a franchise. One was headed by Lorne Duguid, a distiller and a prominent Canadian sportsman. He was with Harold Ballard and Maple Leaf Gardens. Another was the Toronto Baseball Co. Ltd., headed by Syd C. Cooper, with Montreal financier Howard Webster.

Webster had been involved peripherally with the Montreal Expos when he made a loan (since repaid) to a nephew, Lorne Webster, to invest in the Expos in 1967. Twice in the early 1970s the Montreal financier attempted to acquire a National League franchise for Toronto. In 1971 he met with San Diego Padres' C. Arnholt Smith and made an attractive offer that was later turned down.

He made a similar offer in 1972 but again was thwarted. Early in 1975, however, Webster and McDougall formed a partnership through the efforts of Gerry Snyder, who'd also helped obtain the NL franchise for Montreal.

In September of 1975 an inter-league committee of baseball was reported to have suggested Toronto as a possible site for relocating the Giants. They were in deep financial trouble because of declining attendance at San Francisco's Candlestick Park. The team had borrowed $500,000 from the league and was in debt to the banks for $1 million.

Later in September McDougall confirmed a story that his company met representatives of the Giants in San Francisco to discuss Labatt's possible purchase of the team. McDougall said owner Horace Stoneham wanted Labatt's to accept the team's responsibilities in the city if the sale were made. This meant paying about $4.5 million to buy the Giants out of the 18 years remaining on the 35-year lease.

On January 9, 1976, it was announced that Labatt's, Vulcan Assets and the CIBC had reached "an agreement in principle" to purchase the Giants for $13.5 million and to move them to Toronto for the 1976 season.

Two days later, George Moscone, newly elected mayor of the west coast city, announced he would fight to keep the Giants. The following day he obtained a temporary restraining order against the move to Toronto.

Meanwhile in Phoenix at an owner's meeting the Labatt's group, headed by McDougall, Ontario sales manager David Cashen and lawyer Herb Solway, made their presentation. The league was unable to vote because of the injunction.

Early in February Judge John Everett Benson listened to both sides and announced he would "take the case under advisement." With the restraining order still on, Mayor Moscone brought forth buyers for the club: One being Giants' director Robert Lurie, another Robert Short of Minneapolis, who had previously owned major league teams in Washington and Texas.

Former major league infielder and coach and one of minor league's outstanding managers, Roy Hartsfield, Blue Jays' field boss.

Batting instructor Bobby Doerr of Blue Jays is former all-star second baseman of the Red Sox.

Far left: Blue Jays' pitching coach is Bob Miller, who pitched for 10 major league teams. Managed last year.

Judge Benson delayed his decision. The Lurie-Short offer of $8 million was accepted after much discussion by NL officials. However, Toronto almost got the Giants later that month when Short backed out of the deal. Despite missing the March 1 deadline for payment, Lurie at the last hour came up with another investor in Phoenix, Ariz., meat packer Bud Herseth.

Toronto was out–but not for long.

The American League, which had eyed Toronto since the turn of the century, met in Tampa, Fla., on March 21 and decided on expansion.

A new group, headed by Phil and Irving Granovsky, along with David Dennis, Fred McCutcheon and James F. Kay, suddenly emerged and said it was after the Toronto franchise.

But MacPhail and the American League went with the McDougall consortium. They had been in it from the start and had done all the "leg work."

It took more than a month for the AL to give its final approval because of commissioner Kuhn's efforts to give the NL more time to consider its earlier rejection of expansion into Toronto. MacPhail flew into Toronto April 27 with league executives to make it official.

McDougall was elated.

"The period from September of '74 to today was filled with drama that was certainly unexpected but in retrospect not unenjoyable. Our greatest disappointment had to be the court decision in San Francisco which enjoined the owners of the Giants from making the sale that would move the club to Toronto.

"Our greatest frustration was with the National League owners and their inability to decide on expansion. The climax came when their president, Chub Feeney, invited me to make a presentation. I did. Following the presentation they voted 8-4 in favor of expansion but the NL constitution requires an unanimous vote to approve such a move.

"After a recess and further discussion, the meeting reconvened. This time the vote was 9-3. Another recess, more debate and a further vote of 10-2 but still little prospect for unanimity.

"Finally, the chairman at the suggestion of an owner opposed to expansion, asked for a motion to adjourn. The meeting began to break up until someone called for a vote. Believe it or not, for the first time in history I suspect, a motion to adjourn was defeated.

"Now you had the unusual circumstance of a group of powerful men locked in a room with not enough votes to adjourn but not enough votes to decide the issue.

"After several more hours, they resolved this dilemma with a two-week postponement. Frustration–not only for us but also for our friends in the National League."

Webster, who preferred to maintain a low profile throughout the many negotiations, said, "With the expansion team we at least have more time to set things up. It would have been a rush if we succeeded in buying the Giants. Now we can look closely at possible coaches and farm teams. We have a lot to learn."

Recently both McDougall and Cashen voiced similar opinions.

"In light of subsequent events we are lucky that the Giants' purchase didn't happen, even though we gave it our best shot," said McDougall.

Given the extra year, the Toronto group was able to structure its new organization to its own specifications, instead of having to take over the skeleton of the Giants and try to patch up things as they went wrong.

It also meant that instead of paying $13.5 million for the Giants–$8 million for the team and the rest to pay for costs of litigation to break Candlestick Park's lease–they got an expansion franchise for $7 million.

Cashen said, "Having endured all the frustrations of the Giants' situation, it feels kind of nice that our objective of bringing major league ball to Toronto was achieved. I'm pleased that Toronto and the stadium had an extra year to prepare and I think the whole thing is looking more professional than if we'd tried to rush through the transfer of the Giants."

Shortly the pieces began to fall into place.

Webster was named chairman of the board of Metro Baseball Ltd., official name of the Blue Jays, with Labatt's vice-president Peter Hardy vice-chairman. Other directors named were McDougall, David A. Lewis, senior vice-president of the CIBC and John Robarts, former Ontario premier and a member of a Toronto law firm.

Metro voted 27-3 to spend $2.8 million to complete renovation and enlargement of Exhibition Place Stadium. The club (it wasn't the Blue Jays yet) hired its first employees: Paul Beeston, an accountant from London, Ont., who was named vice-president, administration; Howie Starkman, former publicity director of the hockey Maple Leafs and Bobby Hewitson, former front office official of the baseball Maple Leafs.

But the major acquisition of the McDougall group was Peter Bavasi, vice-president and general manager of the San Diego Padres of the NL. Bavasi, 34, is the son of Padres' president and former Los Angeles and Brooklyn Dodger general manager, Buzzy Bavasi.

He has been involved in baseball administration for 12 years and is graduated with a BA in philosophy from St. Mary's College at Moraga, Calif. He received a 5-year contract.

Bavasi, executive vice-president and general manager, added to his staff Pat Gillick and Elliott Wahle, key men in the New York Yankees' farm system. Gillick, 38, was handed the role of vice-president, player personnel. Wahle was named administrator of player personnel. Gillick had spent 13 years in the Houston Astros and Yankee organizations.

The club also selected Dunedin, Fla., as its training base. The team nickname came from more than 30,000 responses and 4,000 different names submitted in a name the team contest.

There were suggestions to call the team everything from the Dingbats, Towers, Hogtowners, Trilliums and Dons to the Blue Sox, Blues, Maple Leafs, Beer Bellies, Bootleggers and Blue Bats. Blue Jays won out and within a few months the name had "grown" on fans after first receiving a critical welcome.

Blue Jays' next move was to hire a manager. The man was Roy Thomas Hartsfield, who had spent 33 years in baseball, a minor league manager with an exceptional record, especially with the Hawaii Islanders and Spokane of the Pacific Coast League.

A major league infielder with the Boston Braves, Hartsfield had also been a coach with the Los Angeles Dodgers and Atlanta Braves.

In the ensuing weeks came announcements that Bobby Doerr, a former all-star second baseman with the Boston Red Sox, had been signed as batting instructor. Bob Miller, who pitched for 10 different big league teams, was pitching coach. Other coaches signed were Don Leppert, Harry Warner and Jackie Moore, a catcher who managed the Maple Leafs for their final four games before the club folded in 1967.

The next act was the biggest one: the club acquired a team.

Before the AL's expansion draft the only players on the roster were veteran catcher Phil Roof, who had been with the Maple Leafs in 1963, and three ex-Padres from the Hawaii team – Dave Hilton, John Scott and Dave Roberts.

On November 5 in the Terrace Room of the elegant Plaza Hotel in New York the Blue Jays were created. Joe Cronin, chairman of the American League, presented Webster and Bavasi with a certificate of membership in the 76-year-old organization before Danny Kaye, the comedian and part-owner of the Seattle Mariners, and Bavasi made their clubs' first draft selections.

As expected Kaye selected Ruppert Jones. At 10:31 a.m. Bavasi announced "The Toronto Blue Jays select from the Baltimore Orioles...Robert M. Bailor."

In the next seven hours the Blue Jays selected 29 more players from the 12 existing franchises at a cost of $175,000 apiece.

Their final selection of the draft was Leon Hooten of Oakland, a pitcher with a 5.60 ERA and 2-8 won-lost record.

Before the day was over one of the Blue Jays' second round selections was traded in a 2-for-1 transaction. Later, at the winter meetings in Los Angeles in December, another new Blue Jay, Rico Carty, was traded for two younger players.

There were to be considerable more deals and drafts before opening day, 1977, against the Chicago White Sox.

But it finally has happened. Toronto is in the big leagues of baseball. The game so many love is back in town.

Robert M. Bailor	shortstop	Baltimore
Theodore (Jerry) Garvin	pitcher	Minnesota
James Clancy	pitcher	Texas
Gary Lee Woods	outfielder	Oakland
Ricardo Carty	designated hitter	Cleveland

(Traded in December to Cleveland for outfielder John Lowenstein and catcher Rick Cerone)

Claude Edge	pitcher	Milwaukee
Al Fitzmorris	pitcher	Kansas City

(Traded on day of draft to Cleveland for catcher Al Ashby and first baseman Doug Howard)

Alvis Woods	outfielder	Minnesota
Michael E. Darr	pitcher	Baltimore
Peter D. Vuckovich	pitcher	Chicago
Jeffrey A. Byrd	pitcher	Texas
Stephen S. Bowling	outfielder	Milwaukee
Dennis DeBarr	pitcher	Detroit
William Singer	pitcher	Minnesota
James P. Mason	shortstop	New York
Douglas Ault	first baseman	Texas
Ernest L. Whitt	catcher	Boston
Stephan M. Weathers	second baseman	Oakland
Stephen Staggs	second baseman	Kansas City
Steven Lowell Hargan	pitcher	Texas
Garth Iorg	second baseman	New York
David L. Lemanczyk	pitcher	Detroit
Lawrence D. Anderson	pitcher	Milwaukee

(Sent to Chicago in January to complete Roof deal)

Jesse D. Jefferson	pitcher	Chicago
David Lawrence McKay	infielder	Minnesota
Thomas M. Bruno	pitcher	Kansas City
Otoniel Velez	outfielder	New York
Michael H. Willis	pitcher	Baltimore
Samuel J. Ewing	designated hitter	Chicago
Michael Leon Hooten	pitcher	Oakland

Previously Signed

Philip A. Roof	catcher	Chicago
David W. Roberts	catcher	Hawaii

(Traded to San Diego in February for pitcher Jerry Johnson)

John D. Hilton	third baseman	Hawaii
John Henry Scott	outfielder	Hawaii

A similar scene
but 26 years later.
At left Brooklyn
Dodger vice-president
E. J. (Buzzie) Bavasi signs
Don (Big Newk) Newcombe
to a reported $20,000 contract.
Peter Bavasi, Buzzie's son and
vice-president of the Blue
Jays, goes over contract with
ex-Dodger pitcher Bill
Singer, who Toronto drafted
from Minnesota Twins.

Jays drafted Jim Mason,
lone Yankee to hit a homer in
1976 World Series.

Toronto's No. 1 draft choice,
Bob Bailor, a promising
young shortstop.

195

Pitcher Dave Lemanczyk,
who won four games for the
Detroit Tigers in 1976.

Otto Velez, an outfielder and
designated hitter selected
from the Yanks.

Pedro Garcia dives through
air after collision with
Kansas City's Tom Poquette
at second base. He was with
Tigers and Brewers in 1976.

Southpaw Mike Willis won 12
games for Rochester in the
1976 season.

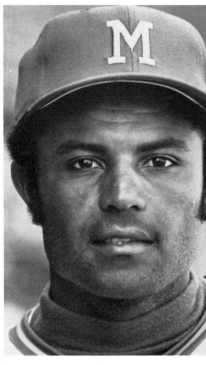

One of the coveted young catchers in
baseball is former Indian Alan Ashby.

Another of Blue Jays' young backstops
is Rick Cerone, obtained in Carty trade.

Fiery Pedro Garcia led American League
in doubles for Brewers with 32 in 1973.

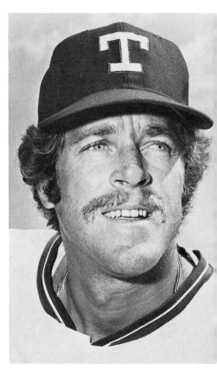

Tom Bruno, a young righthander drafted
from Kansas City had a 1-0 mark.

Sam Ewing, selected from Chicago, is a
designated hitter candidate.

Steve Hargan won eight games with Texas
in 1976 and more than 80 in majors.

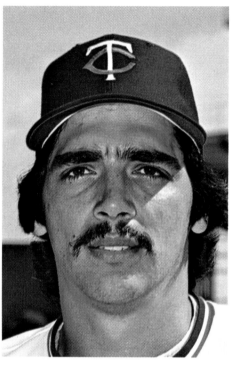

Jefferson was both a starter and
...fer for White Sox in 1976.

Dave McKay, a Canadian, is a strong
candidate for third baseman's job.

Steve Staggs led American Association
in games and hit .283 for Omaha in 1976.

...Lowenstein can play almost any
...ion. Was with Indians last season.

Bill Singer, who pitched no-hitter for
Dodgers, was 13-10 last season.

Pete Vuckovich appeared in 33 games
with Chicago in 1976 and was 7-4.

Bibliography

General Reference Books

Bob Broeg
Super Stars of Baseball
The Sporting News Publishing Co., St. Louis, Mo., 1971

Richard M. Cohen, David S. Neft, Roland T. Johnson & Jordan A. Deutsch
The World Series
New York: The Dial Press, 1976

Richard Grossinger
Baseball Issue IO Publications, Cape Elizabeth, Me.

Nancy and Maxwell L. Howell
Sports and Games In Canadian Life, 1700 to the Present
Macmillan of Canada, 1969

Irving A. Leitner
Baseball: Diamond In The Rough
Criterion Books,
published by Abelard-Schuman Ltd., New York – London, 1972

David S. Neft, Roland T. Johnson, Richard M. Cohen & Jordan A. Deutsch
The Sports Encyclopedia: Baseball
New York: Grosset & Dunlap, 1976

Robert Obojski
Bush League: A History Of Minor League Baseball
New York: Macmillan Publishing Company, Inc., 1975

David R. Phillips and Lawrence Kart
That Old Ball Game
Chicago: Henry Regnery Company, 1975

A Rutledge Book
A Baseball Century: New York
Macmillan Publishing Co. Inc., 1976

Robert Smith
Illustrated History of Baseball: New York
Grosset & Dunlap, Inc., 1973

Hy Turkin and S. C. Thompson
The Official Encyclopedia of Baseball (Jubilee Edition)
A. S. Barnes & Co., New York, 1951

Wells Twombly
200 Years Of Sport In America
A Rutledge Book, McGraw-Hill Book Company, 1976

S. F. Wise and Douglas Fisher for Canada's Hall of Fame
Canada's Sporting Heroes
Don Mills, Ontario: General Publishing Company Limited, 1974

Min S. Yee and Donald K. Wright
The Sports Book
Bantam Books, Inc., Toronto – New York – London, 1975

Magazines and Periodicals

Stephen J. Gamester
Maclean's Flashback. August 22nd, 1964

Stan Grosshandler
The American League's Opening Season, 1901

International League of Professional Baseball Clubs
White Book, 40th edition, Rochester, N.Y.
Published by the International League, 1976

Henry H. Roxborough
Sport In Early Toronto
(The Sandlot Game; When Diamonds were a Man's Best Friend).

Controlled Media Corporation Inc.
is deeply appreciative
of the involvement of
Labatt Breweries of Canada Ltd.,
and the
Canadian Imperial Bank of Commerce
in the publication of this book.

since
1828

Labatt's is pleased
to have played a part in bringing
the Blue Jays to Toronto.

Enjoy the game.
Enjoy the book.

Don McDougall

The Commerce
Major League – Worldwide